FARROW&BALL
DECORATING
with COLOUR

Farrow&Ball
DECORATING
with COLOUR

Ros Byam Shaw

photography by
Jan Baldwin

RYLAND PETERS & SMALL
LONDON • NEW YORK

Senior designer Toni Kay
Commissioning editor Annabel Morgan
Location research Jess Walton
Production manager Gordana Simakovic
Art director Leslie Harrington
Editorial director Julia Charles

First published in 2013
by Ryland Peters & Small
20–21 Jockey's Fields,
London WC1R 4BW
and
519 Broadway, 5th Floor
New York, NY 10012
www.rylandpeters.com

10 9 8 7 6 5 4 3 2 1

ISBN 978 1 84975 423 1

A catalogue record for this book is
available from the British Library.

US Library of Congress cataloging-in-
publication data has been applied for.

Printed and bound in China

*Please note that paint and wallpaper
colours may vary due to the printing
process. We recommend using tester
pots and swatches to check all
colours in situ.*

*All colours and paint names are
trademarks of Farrow & Ball
Holdings Ltd.*

PAGE 1 Archive colour 'Saxon Green'.
PAGE 2 'Manor House Gray'.
PAGE 3 'Cinder Rose'.
THIS PAGE Archive colour 'Berrington Blue'.
OPPOSITE, CLOCKWISE FROM TOP LEFT
'Charleston Gray'; Archive colour 'Saxon
Green'; 'Orangerie' wallpaper BP2501
with woodwork in 'White Tie'.

CONTENTS

INTRODUCTION

Like *Downton Abbey* and cricket, Savile Row tailoring and roast beef, Farrow & Ball paints and wallpapers are a great British export. Since the original Mr Farrow and Mr Ball began mixing pigment in Dorset in the 1940s, the company has grown to become a global brand. From acorn to oak, while spreading its branches all the way over the ocean to America, and across the channel to mainland Europe, Farrow & Ball has always stayed true to its roots; its products still made in Dorset by craftsmen, still formulated with traditional ingredients, and still bearing memorable names, whether that old favourite 'Dead Salmon' or more recent additions such as 'Charlotte's Locks' and 'Mizzle'.

Having already written a book about houses decorated using Farrow & Ball, I thought I knew their products well and had seen the full range of their decorative effects. As well as writing about their paints, I had used and lived with them myself for the past 25 years. But all the locations featured in the previous book, *Farrow & Ball Living with Colour*, were English, and travelling for this book to France, Germany, Holland, Italy, Denmark, Norway, and Switzerland to meet designers, architects, and home owners who are fans of Farrow & Ball has been a revelation. There is immediate recognition of the brand as both British and well established, but the historical or heritage associations that still attach to the colours and designs in their country of origin resonate less strongly. This shift of emphasis means the products are appreciated purely for their quality and the range, depth, and subtlety of their colours, and are used accordingly.

Again and again, I heard praise for the matt, chalky finish of Estate Emulsion and the way it gives colour an almost three-dimensional, sensuous feel. One interior decorator, Eva Gnaedinger, described how a visiting friend had exclaimed that the 'Shaded White' on her walls looked so soft that she wanted to lie on it and go to sleep. Equally appreciated are the colours themselves, which are considered stylish, intriguing, reliably pleasing, and just as appropriate for contemporary schemes and buildings as they are for period ones. In fact, the distinction seems to be almost irrelevant. A good colour is a good colour, and the fact that it is based on a paint found under later layers in an English stately home, or on the shade of grey of ancient limewash, has no bearing on how you might choose to use it in the 21st century. Marco Lobina, who is a stockist for Farrow & Ball in Turin, and whose taste could not be more uncompromisingly modern, has used paints and wallpapers in a completely original and surprising way that proves definitively how 'traditional' colours and patterns can be employed to create interiors that are so fashion-forward that they verge on the futuristic.

Most of the houses and apartments in this book, whether in cities, towns, villages, or surrounded by fields, are furnished with a mix of the old and the new. A few lean heavily in one direction or the other, but a healthy hybrid is the norm. The common factor that ensures this mix works is an individual and confident sense of style. This is true even for the houses that have been decorated on a strict budget, such as Eva Gnaedinger's. Quality of design and manufacture is recognized and appreciated by these people, and this is the third characteristic of Farrow & Ball paints and wallpapers that is always commented on. 'The paint has the feel of something that has been made by hand – both simple and beautiful,' says Antonello Radi, himself a patron and exporter of Italian craftsmanship and vernacular skills. 'You can tell that the wallpapers are made with real love and care because they have such character,' says decorator Maud Steengracht, whose home office in the Dutch countryside is lined with 'Versailles' and 'Orangerie' papers.

This has been an exciting book to research and write. It is possible that the rest of Europe is a little more adventurous than Britain when it comes to the decoration of its homes. Certainly wallpaper is more popular, and so is the work of contemporary artists and designers, which finds its place alongside antiques as naturally as we might pair an Aga range cooker with a painted dresser. The creativity of each of the home owners and interior decorators, allied with the cultural differences between countries – sometimes obvious, sometimes slight – make for a variety of architectural styles and heterogeneity of interior design. On one page you will find a log cabin in the Norwegian mountains, on another a palazzo in Umbria. There is a house in Paris conjured from an old fur factory and an apartment in the same city in the attic of an 18th-century *hôtel particulier*. There are family houses and bachelor pads, country farms and urban villas. A love of Farrow & Ball links them all.

Ros Byam Shaw

PAGE 6 Walls of 'Blue Ground' in the foreground, 'Joa's White' beyond, and 'Porphyry Pink' beyond that.
PAGE 7 Walls painted 'Off-White' with a tabletop in 'Off-Black'.
ABOVE LEFT Cupboards painted 'Mouse's Back' with a door in 'London Clay' and walls and ceiling in 'Shaded White'.
LEFT A wall painted 'Mahogany' with 'Stony Ground' beyond.
OPPOSITE A dresser in 'Mouse's Back'.
OVERLEAF 'Charlotte's Locks' above wooden panelling.

STYLE & DECORATION

CLASSIC

These five Northern European homes, two in London, two in Germany and one in Oslo, share the high ceilings, vertical fenestration, and detailing that characterize classical architecture. However, within this traditional framework, each owner has come up with a markedly individual style of decoration, from the striking, contemporary artworks that punctuate Mamuka Bliadze's grandly proportioned rooms to the refined antique furnishings of a London mansion flat. Farrow & Ball paints and wallpapers create the ideal background for them all.

ABOVE 'Lotus' BP2007 wallpaper **OPPOSITE** Walls painted in 'Dix Blue'

THIS PAGE At one end of the open-plan kitchen and dining room is a more formal seating area, separated by a screen wall. The neutral scheme of walls in 'Shaded White' Estate Emulsion and woodwork in 'Wimborne White' Estate Eggshell continues throughout the space, including the kitchen. The theatrical portraits to the left of the fireplace are by Billy & Hells.

A house is never perfect. Even if you start from scratch and build something bespoke, you are still constrained by planning restrictions, building regulations, and the demands of the site. But sometimes a house suits its occupants so ideally that it can seem almost perfect. This is true of this handsome villa, built in 1925, on the outskirts of a pretty medieval town in Southern Germany, which is the home of Maria, Frank, and their two young children, Elisabeth and Leopold.

ABOVE The drama of the entrance hall, with its original parquet floor and sweeping staircase, is accentuated by the 'Pitch Black' of the woodwork and stair banisters set against walls in 'Hardwick White'. The pair of arched, glazed double doors adds to the architectural aplomb of the space, one leading to an entrance lobby, the other to a cloakroom.

PRACTICAL POISE

The location is ideal: close to the children's school and the hospital where Maria works as a psychiatrist, quiet but within walking distance of the town centre. The accommodation is ideal: a garden with space to play and to grow vegetables; a big, open-plan kitchen, dining, and living room; upstairs, suites of rooms for parents and children, and a shared office for Maria and Frank; guest and au-pair bedrooms on the floor above. In the basement there is storage space and a sauna.

'We love it to bits and pieces,' beams Maria. 'And we feel very lucky to have found it. We had been looking for so long and were just about to give up and settle in Munich, where Frank's family business is based. But the minute we walked through the door of this house, we knew it was the place for us. It was instant.' Any visitor to the house would understand Frank and Maria's *coup de foudre*. The entrance hall is a glorious space, with arched, glazed doors and parquet flooring.

THIS PICTURE Looking across the dining room table, from the kitchen end of this large, bright room, the view through to the sitting room is protected by the screen wall papered on both sides in 'Lotus' BP2007 wallpaper, translating the 'Shaded White' of the walls and 'Wimborne White' of the woodwork into pattern and texture, and giving the architectural device of the room divider its own decorative status. The wall on the left marks one edge of the large, window-lined bay, which was originally a separate garden room and is painted 'Castle Gray'.

The sweeping staircase has unusually stylish banisters like chunky musical notes rising towards the landing under a curving, carved handrail.

It may have been love at first sight, but it wasn't entirely unconditional love. Maria and Frank recognized that there were changes they wanted to make, and that they would need help to make them. 'Fortunately, we already knew Barbara, who is a wonderful interior decorator and has a beautiful shop,' Maria explains. 'Barbara has a great sense of aesthetics, but she is also very intuitive, and really tries to understand what a client likes, and needs, from a home. We did a lot of talking about layout and how we would use the space, then she came up with a plan for each room. We wanted an interior

that was highly practical, but also a little bit glamorous – not the blank white walls typical of many German interiors.'

The relationship between Barbara and Maria seems more like one of old friends than client and decorator. When they discuss the changes they made to the house, they generously give each other credit. 'The family love colour and pattern, and have strong ideas about what they like, which makes them a pleasure to work with,' Barbara enthuses, and Maria praises Barbara for her skill at running a team of builders, as well as her creative abilities.

The house had already evolved to suit a more modern lifestyle, but Frank and Maria have made further adjustments to bring it up to date, while reinstating some lost period features, such as cornices.

OPPOSITE A rear hall divides the new open-plan kitchen from the much smaller original kitchen which, with its fitted cupboards and drawers, is now used as a utility room. The traditional encaustic tiles, or *Zementfliesen*, in greens and blues, inspired much of the colour scheme for the house, including the 'Card Room Green' used here for the walls above dado level, complemented by fresh 'Wimborne White'.

ABOVE LEFT AND RIGHT The custom-built kitchen cupboards are painted 'Wimborne White', as is the woodwork and the wall-mounted shelves, against walls in 'Shaded White'. The marble-topped table beside the window offers a place for more informal meals.

OPPOSITE When working from home, Frank and Maria share this first-floor office. As elsewhere, woodwork and shelves are 'Wimborne White', a colour that ensures a visual link between rooms on all four floors. Walls are 'Lamp Room Gray', an elegant and sophisticated background for the businesslike clutter of computers, phones, files, and storage boxes. The delicate chandelier adds an unexpected dash of glamour.

LEFT 'Bumble Bee' BP547 wallpaper in lustrous gold on green brings a taste of luxury to the smallest room in the house – the downstairs cloakroom.

BELOW LEFT 'Bumble Bee' in the same colourway makes a second appearance on the first floor, in the lobby that separates the children's bedrooms. The matchboarding and woodwork are 'Wimborne White', and the 'Setting Plaster' pink of the walls in Elisabeth's bedroom can be glimpsed through the open door.

BELOW RIGHT The walls in Leopold's bedroom are 'Oval Room Blue'. The depth and subtlety of this blue and the plaster pink of Elisabeth's walls are a far cry from the cloying shades of pastel so often allotted to girls and boys, and prevents their choice from seeming obvious or clichéd.

LEFT AND ABOVE Upstairs, Barbara has rearranged the space to give Frank and Maria a suite of rooms, including a dressing room each. Frank's dressing room is between the bedroom and bathroom and has fitted cupboards in 'Charleston Gray'. The bathroom walls are 'Cornforth White' and the woodwork is 'Wimborne White'.

OPPOSITE The wall behind the bedhead is papered in 'Bamboo' BP2105. Behind this wall, Barbara has taken a slice out of the room to create a dressing room for Maria.

Designed for an era when even modest households had at least one servant, the original kitchen was tucked away behind the staircase. This relatively small room, with its floor-to-ceiling fitted cupboards and drawers, is now a spacious and practical utility room. On the other side of the house, where there would once have been three separate reception rooms and a conservatory, walls have been removed to make a single, large open-plan space, with the new kitchen situated at one end. The elegant dining room now extends into the broad, glazed bay of the old conservatory, and at the opposite end to the kitchen is the sitting room. This comfortable and luxurious space, with its fireplace, sofa, and chairs, has been given a degree of separation by the addition of a broad section of wall with wide openings on either side.

The paints throughout are Farrow & Ball. Barbara says she always uses them, and Maria loves the fact that they are eco-friendly. They have also used Farrow & Ball wallpapers: 'Bumble Bee' for the lobby between the children's bedrooms and bathroom and in the cloakroom, 'Bamboo' in the main bedroom, and 'Lotus' on the wall between the dining room and living room. This last use is particularly interesting, as it gives the wall, which partially divides the living room from the dining room, the feel of a decorative screen rather than a structural element. The large-scale 'Lotus' is an ideal choice, not only because it has an Art Deco flavour appropriate to the date of the house, but also because it so successfully bridges the transition from the kitchen and dining area to the more formal sitting area, and is equally at home in both.

DECORATING PRINCIPLE 1

Dark Drama

Decorating with dark colours is counter-intuitive in small or badly-lit spaces, but the results can be wonderfully theatrical and more visually exciting than attempts to create sweetness and light with an all-over coating of white paint. In fact, because dark colours recede, they create an illusion of space, especially if you include ceilings and woodwork. Then there are the opportunities for intriguing visual contrasts – pale paintings floating on moody backgrounds, sculptural furnishings silhouetted, light beyond the darkness.

ABOVE AND BELOW RIGHT Dark colours are traditional for dining rooms because their effect is particularly handsome by candlelight. A more contemporary night-time space is the media room, here doubling as a library (see pages 14–23). Walls and ceiling are painted 'Hague Blue', and the fitted bookshelves are a shade duskier in 'Black Blue'. The effect is cocooning and also glamorous, as befits a private cinema.

CENTRE In a large, bright room, mainly decorated in off-whites and neutrals, this wall painted in velvety 'Off-Black' would almost disappear if it were not for the glow of flames or the flicker of the flat-screen television mounted to the left of the fireplace (see pages 96–103). Framed by a pale colour, neither would have the same visual impact.

OPPOSITE ABOVE RIGHT 'Brinjal' can look strikingly contemporary, or equally appropriate on period panelling, as here. White towels stand out in clean, crisp contrast.

OPPOSITE BELOW RIGHT James van der Velden has painted the windowless entrance hall of his attic flat (see pages 74–79) in 'Mahogany', emphasizing the light and space in the rooms that lead off it.

OPPOSITE ABOVE LEFT TO RIGHT
The house dates from the early 18th century, but the façade and front door have been returned to how they would have looked in 1820, before the addition of a shop front that John dismantled and removed. The exterior woodwork is 'Green Smoke' eggshell, and the render below the ground-floor windows is 'Off-Black'.

OPPOSITE BELOW The front window of the kitchen is below street level, but the room gains light from French doors that lead onto the garden. When John first bought the house, this basement was filled with rubble. Now fully restored, complete with flagstones and matchboard panelling, its woodwork in 'Card Room Green' and walls in 'String', it is hard to believe the room has not been in continuous, comfortable use

for the past 300 years. Bringing it up to date are modernist furnishings, including the chair in the foreground, which John found on the street.

RIGHT The working end of the kitchen is at the front of the house and is fitted with robust cupboards that were recycled from an old garage and given a coat of 'Card Room Green'. The matchboarding on the walls is 'String'.

BELOW RIGHT Open-plan living is a recent innovation and the kitchen would originally have been two rooms. The doorway between them remains, without its door, and another wider opening, seen here, also links the spaces. The divide is marked by the change from panelling and plaster in 'String' on the left to 'Card Room Green' on the right.

AGEING GRACEFULLY

When John Nicolson was a boy growing up in Glasgow, he was fascinated by a deserted mansion opposite his school. 'The two old ladies who lived there had died, and it was abandoned', he remembers. 'I found a way to get in. It was very Miss Havisham. Some of the furnishings had been left – huge, old pieces of Victoriana – and there were leather-bound books in the library and a mangle in the kitchen. We lived in a tenement building and I begged my parents to buy the house. I wanted them to rescue it.'

John Nicolson is a broadcaster and journalist who will be familiar to viewers of British news and current affairs programmes, including the BBC's *Breakfast News*. Throughout his media career, he has retained his childhood love of old buildings, and what he describes as 'sympathy and compassion for houses that are derelict, abandoned, and unloved.' 'When I was looking for somewhere to live in London in the 1990s,'

he expands, 'Spitalfields, in East London, was incredibly run-down – no one wanted to live here – but I loved the early 18th-century architecture, and spotted this house, which was empty. I wrote to the Land Registry to find out who owned it and if I could buy it.' So began the house rescue of his boyhood dreams.

The house dates from 1722 – a time when the area's prosperity was dependent on the Huguenot silk weavers who settled here as refugees, fleeing religious persecution in their native France. It had not been lived in since the 1920s and there was no plumbing or electricity, just loops of wiring leading from the electricity

supply outside the front door. The attic had suffered bomb damage in the war and was waterlogged, and the basement was so full of silt and rubble that the only way in was to squeeze through the area window below pavement level.

John moved into the house soon after work began on its restoration. At the time, he was working as a presenter on the BBC's *Watchdog* consumer affairs programme, despite which, or perhaps oblivious to which, his builders proved to be both nefarious and incompetent. 'They kept claiming things had been stolen,' John laughs, 'when in fact they were taking the stuff themselves.

ABOVE The ground floor was originally divided into two rooms, each with its own fireplace. Now a single space, it is used as a study with a fitted desk at the back overlooking the garden, and as a dining room at the front. All the original features had been stripped out, but John reinstated the 18th-century feel of the room with chimneypieces and matchboard panelling, painted in 'Light Gray', and walls above in 'Off-White'. The Eames La Chaise was one of his more triumphant junk-shop finds, its space-age modernism in pleasing contrast with the period setting.

THIS PAGE Sitting on the dado rail next to the fireplace at the dining end of the room are white ceramic letters once used to spell out the story in early silent films. The Arts and Crafts chair was found on the street.

JohN

Eventually they were arrested, and I found new builders, who were very good.' In the midst of the chaos, John made himself a small oasis on the top floor, complete with a newly plumbed bathroom, and lived on takeaway bagels and breakfasts at the burger bar round the corner. 'I would come down in my suit in the morning, picking my way through the filth, breathing in clouds of dust, and then attempt to appear calm and immaculate in front of the cameras.'

Filth, dust, and domestic upheaval aside, John relished the restoration. 'It was like opening a Russian doll. The early Georgian fabric of the house had been buried under later layers. On the first floor, there were sheets of metal cladding that had been installed in the 19th century as a crude sort of fireproofing. Behind it was original panelling.' Many of the architectural features had survived, including the staircase with its beautifully turned banisters. The front of the house, however, had been altered in the 1820s when a shop front was added that spanned the ground floor of the house next door. As it was neither complete nor original, it was decided that it would be better to remove it.

The façade was returned to its pre-shop-front appearance, but part of the shop front itself was recycled as the dining-room table, made up from the old wood by a local joiner. 'That wood is now in its fourth incarnation – tree, ship, shop front, dining table,' says John, who explains that many of the houses in Spitalfields were built using timber from redundant ships. Rescuing and recycling is a theme.

OPPOSITE The apple-green upholstery of the vintage dining chairs is fresh and bright against the smoky 'Light Gray' of the dining-room panelling.

ABOVE RIGHT John has left the early Georgian staircase uncarpeted. Its untouched feel is enhanced by a palette of 'drab' colours, similar to those that might originally have been used in the house: 'Tanner's Brown', 'London Clay', and 'London Stone' for the woodwork, 'Stony Ground' for the wall plaster, and 'Off-White' for the ceiling.

RIGHT The attic bedroom has fitted cupboards in 'Mouse's Back', to the apparent delight of ginger cat Rojo.

THIS PAGE Walls in the Archive colour 'Berrington Blue' above panelling in 'Lamp Room Gray' have a later Georgian feel that is appropriate for the master bedroom, which was 'updated' towards the end of the 18th century. The wardrobe was made by local joiner Dave Thompson, copied from a design by early Victorian architect Alexander 'Greek' Thomson, and is painted in 'Railings'.

The dining room is also home to a large, glass-fronted 19th-century cabinet, which John found discarded on a local street. In the drawing room is an Ercol sofa also found on the street. The same is true of a chair in the second-floor bedroom and the butcher's block in the basement kitchen, where the fitted cupboards were once storage in an old garage. Blinds from neighbour Marianna Kennedy are another instance of creative reuse – they are made from 1940s bookbinding linen. Even the bead-and-butt panelling in the attic bathroom once lined a Victorian back extension, now demolished.

John says his aim was to give the impression that the house had always been looked after, and had aged gracefully, 'like a fine old actor who hasn't had any "work" done'. Farrow & Ball paints, with their 'knocked-back' feel, help to promote the illusion. As for the colours he has chosen – which range from dusky 'Brinjal' in a bathroom and bright 'Berrington Blue' for a bedroom to earthy 'Tanner's Brown',

'London Clay', and 'London Stone' for the staircase – he says he did not choose them on the grounds of authenticity, but because they are colours he loves.

Although John has restored the architecture of the house with meticulous attention to period detail, the furnishings are no period pastiche. In the main bedroom, a bed made by designer Tom Dixon for a Japanese pop star who changed his mind about wanting it sits next to a wardrobe copied from a design by 19th-century Glasgow architect Alexander 'Greek' Thomson. In the dining room, the amoebic curves of an Eames La Chaise chair sit against traditional tongue-and-groove panelling, while on the landing a 1960s Italian chandelier casts shadows across the Georgian floorboards.

Rescued and resplendent, the house is once again a home, to John and his partner, academic Juliano Zini. Not surprisingly, it is in hot demand as a location for fashion and interiors shoots. And John also owns a mansion in Glasgow.

ABOVE Against the rich background of 'Brinjal', the furniture and fittings of the attic bathroom stand out in sharp, chic contrast.

BELOW Honky sits by the back door, which opens into the garden designed by Luis Buitrago.

NORTHERN BRIGHTS

Liv and Jan Krogstad live in a first-floor apartment full of colour and contemporary art in Oslo. After 20 years in England, where their children went to school, they moved back to Southern Norway. More recently, they decided that a city apartment would better suit their semi-retirement. 'We had quite strict criteria,' Liv recalls. 'We wanted to be close to shops and to be able to walk to the centre of Oslo, and we wanted somewhere that felt spacious without too many rooms. As soon as we stepped through the door of this apartment, I said "This is it." It turned out it had once belonged to the parents of friends of ours. That is how small a country Norway is!'

ABOVE The entrance hall has its own corner fireplace but no windows. Instead, it borrows light through glazed doors that lead into the living room. Liv and Jan decided to make this space as warm and welcoming as possible with a bold use of 'Blazer', which covers walls and woodwork from skirting/baseboard to picture rail.

LEFT AND OPPOSITE 'Blazer' continues into the study, which leads off the hall. Here the effect is less all-enveloping, as a wall of cupboards on one side and bookshelves on the other are painted in 'All White', which also outlines the door.

In terms of population, Norway is small. In terms of area, however, it is huge – a great slice of densely wooded, mountainous natural beauty, its long coast frilled by fjords, its interior slashed with the silver streaks of innumerable lakes and rivers. In common with many Norwegian city dwellers, Liv and Jan also have a *hytte*, a retreat in the mountains about three hours' drive from Oslo, and featured in the 'Country' chapter of this book (see pages 144–151). The contrast between these two homes could not be more striking. But one thing both have in common is their uplifting use of colour.

The Oslo apartment dates from the 1930s, and although it does not have the feel of a space that has been greatly altered, Liv and Jan have actually reorganized the layout substantially. A small kitchen

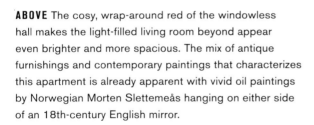

ABOVE The cosy, wrap-around red of the windowless hall makes the light-filled living room beyond appear even brighter and more spacious. The mix of antique furnishings and contemporary paintings that characterizes this apartment is already apparent with vivid oil paintings by Norwegian Morten Slettemeås hanging on either side of an 18th-century English mirror.

and maid's room have become a study and second bathroom, and a new kitchen has been installed at one end of the dining room. Their other major change was to rationalize the entrance and lobby to make a generous hall, now incorporating an original corner fireplace that once warmed a small, separate sitting room. The resulting arrangement – a kitchen and dining room opening into a living room and library beyond, a main bedroom with its own dressing room and bathroom, and a study and spare bathroom at the back – is so practical that it is hard to imagine it ever having been otherwise.

THIS PAGE The living room is divided from the dining room by original sliding doors. The Archive colour 'Buff' provides a neutral backdrop for a collection of contemporary Norwegian art, including the oil painting by Kjell Erik Killi Olsen on the left. 'Buff' is continued into the dining room, where it has levitated onto the ceiling. Here, the walls are 'Wimborne White', against which hang a pair of paintings by Tor Inge Qvenum.

Next on the agenda was paint. Here Liv and Jan have the advantage of a daughter, Kristin, who studied interior design and worked for English interior decorator Jane Churchill before setting up her own business in Oslo as agent for Farrow & Ball and other British companies, including Forbes & Lomax, Besselink & Jones, and Jason D'Souza. 'We have been using Farrow & Ball paint for a long time, and Kristin always helps us choose,' says Liv.

Mother and daughter share a taste for bold colour. 'The entrance hall to the apartment has no windows,' Liv comments, 'but it does have a fireplace. We decided to use 'Blazer' for the walls and the woodwork because it creates such a welcoming atmosphere. In winter, when you come in from the snow, it feels wonderfully cosy.' They have also used 'Blazer' in the study, here crisply contrasted with white-painted cupboards and woodwork. The Victorian art critic John Ruskin recommended a rich red as an ideal background for oil paintings, and the hall and study, which are hung with some of Liv and Jan's impressive art collection, prove his point.

At the other end of the apartment, Liv and Kristen used an equally intense colour, 'Cook's Blue'. While the hall offers wrap-around warmth and enclosure, this deep, serene shade,

OPPOSITE A modern version of a traditional Norwegian corner fireplace warms the living room. The painting is by Per Enoksson. The coffee table is piled with books about the artists whose work Liv and Jan collect.

TOP Legacies of the 20 years Liv, Jan, and their children spent living in England include this painted bureau bought from Harvey Nichols. The oil painting is by Knut Rose and the sculpture on a plinth, which is also painted in 'Buff' to match the walls, is a bronze by Aase Texmon Rygh. The door is open onto the bedroom.

ABOVE The side of the door that faces into the living room is 'Buff' and the side that faces into the bedroom is 'Cook's Blue', as are the bedroom walls and woodwork. Together the two colours are as harmonious as sea and sand.

as fresh as a late-afternoon summer sky, links the bedroom, dressing room, and bathroom in a seamless sweep of azure. Here the blue is background to paintings of clouds by Norwegian artist Ingeborg Stana, reinforcing the illusion of being cushioned by air and space.

In between these two colour extremes, the interconnecting reception rooms are neutral 'Buff', an Archive colour. These are the rooms where the biggest oil paintings are displayed, and in this light, open area with its large windows, the paintings have space to expand, their colours vibrating against the more retiring background. Liv has been buying art for many years, much of it from Knut Blomstrøm, owner of GAD gallery in Oslo. Her coffee table is piled high with books about artists whose work she admires and collects. Some, such as Jan Saether, are friends, at least one, Håkon Gullvåg, has been commissioned by Norway's royal family, and almost all are Scandinavian.

While the artworks are uncompromisingly contemporary, the furnishings are largely traditional, and show a different side to the couple's taste. Like the Norwegian Vikings, Liv and Jan are anglophiles. Many of the fabrics they have used are English, including the Colefax & Fowler chintz that covers the sofa and armchairs, and the Mulberry paisley of the bedroom curtains and headboard. Jan, whose career has been in shipping, has learned to restore antiques, and some of the 18th-century English tea caddies he collects, and which are dotted around the apartment, are testament to his skill at repair and patination. Among the books on the shelves that curve around the corner wall of the apartment are an anthology of The Beatles, a biography of Diana, Princess of Wales, and the *Oxford Dictionary of Quotations*.

The differences in style, date, and provenance of the things that furnish and decorate this apartment might cause a clash, but doesn't. Colour helps to harmonize them, providing a visual link between the chintz and the abstract paintings in the living room, for example. There are other helpful echoes too, such as the stripes of a pleated silk lampshade against the painted stripes of a painting by Kjell Erik Killi Olsen. Liv has an eye for such things, which Kristin has inherited.

LEFT Liv and Jan's bedroom, bathroom, and dressing room are painted floor to ceiling in 'Cook's Blue', a powerfully intense colour that links the three spaces in a sweep of seamless azure. Like the hall, both the bathroom and the dressing room are without windows, but while 'Blazer' feels like a warm hug, here the effect is fresh and calm, like breathing mountain air.

OPPOSITE The curtains and bed head are covered in a paisley by Mulberry, which Jan and Liv brought with them from their former house, a dense pattern that includes a blue very similar to the shade they chose for the walls. The sky paintings are by Ingeborg Stana and the painting to the left of the window is by Israeli artist Yoel Benharrouche.

DECORATING PRINCIPLE 2

Ways with Woodwork

For more than a century, the presumption when decorating has been that walls should be the preserve of colour while the woodwork should be painted a complementary shade of white, as should ceilings and plasterwork. This has not always been the case – Regency interiors often featured a dark skirting/baseboard, and the Victorians liked woodwork in brown. Recently this colour reversal has been revived, and the results look surprisingly modern.

ABOVE RIGHT An example of how to highlight strong architectural elements can be seen in the hall of this villa in Germany (see pages 14–23), where woodwork in 'Pitch Black' is silhouetted against walls of 'Hardwick White'.

BELOW CENTRE Here we see the reverse of dark woodwork against lighter walls in an apartment in Oslo (see pages 34–41), where 'All White' provides crisp contrast and a visual punctuation mark between the bold red 'Blazer' of this room and the hall beyond.

OPPOSITE The drawing room in John Nicolson's house (see pages 26–33) retains its early 18th-century panelling. Aside from the fireplace, which is 'London Clay', he has given the panelling a coat of 'Joa's White', leaving shadows to outline its three-dimensional quality. Had he chosen to pick out individual panels in another colour, it would have made the room seem smaller, and the panelling itself more complicated, instead of elegantly simple.

RIGHT The exterior woodwork of John Nicolson's house is 'Green Smoke', a colour with the right period feel that blends with the tones of the brickwork to harmonious effect.

THIS PAGE At the foot of the stairs that lead down to the kitchen is a bench given to Karina by her father, which she has painted herself in 'Pitch Black' and upholstered with horsehair from John Boyd. The photographs are by Knut Skjærven and the hand-crafted ceramic lampshades are by Ole Andreason of Aleo Design. Walls are 'All White'.

FAR LEFT Glazed doors open into the hall on the raised ground floor, where there is a pair of demi-lune console tables that Karina has painted 'Off-Black' Full Gloss 'to look like lacquer'. A 'Jeeves' bowler hat lamp hangs above a tree made from coloured telephone wire.

LEFT The staircase between the raised and the lower-ground floor has banister rails painted in 'Off-Black' Full Gloss and are carpeted in charcoal coir matting, creating a graphic contrast with the 'All White' banisters and walls.

GREY SUITS

Karina Bjerregaard Chen speaks such immaculate English that it seems entirely appropriate she should live in an 'English townhouse', albeit one in Denmark. She was educated in England when her mother worked for the Danish Consulate in London, and she has since worked in London herself. More recently, she returned to Denmark with her two young sons, Victor and George, resumed her work in finance for a company based in Copenhagen, and bought this elegant house, which is unusual in Denmark for being part of a terraced square built around a communal garden. 'All the 18th-century buildings in central Copenhagen were designed as apartments,' she explains. 'No one lives in the kind of terraced houses you have in London – they just don't exist.'

ABOVE Karina inherited a chic kitchen in wood and brushed stainless steel from the previous owners of the house but has made it her own. Antique keys, a flat iron, and two eel-catchers decorate an alcove behind the sink.

LEFT A woodburning stove is tucked under the stairs in the kitchen, which has been opened into a single space thanks to the support of new steel beams that are silhouetted against the 'All White' walls. The two concrete-topped tables by Morten Voss can seat up to ten and the candlesticks are by Mogens Lassen.

OPPOSITE Adjoining reception rooms on the raised ground floor are linked by double doors. The room at the front is painted in 'Plummett' and furnished with a mix of inherited antiques and contemporary pieces, such as the lithograph by Pierre Alechinsky and a chandelier by Ole Bent Petersen.

BELOW The original white ceramic stove, known in Denmark as a *Svensk kakkelovn*, has its chimney cleaned by a visiting government chimney sweep once a year. The chair, sofa, and the rhomboid stool are all upholstered in Karina's favourite grey flannel, the chair piped in blue velvet to pick up the blue of the Pierre Frey window blind. A tessellation of IKEA photo frames hangs above the leather sofa seen through the double doors.

The English town houses were built at the beginning of the last century, reputedly as the result of a game of cards between the playboy British King Edward VII, who was married to Princess Alexandra of Denmark, and a Danish Count. The King won 70 acres of countryside on the edge of Copenhagen, and sold it to the English insurance company Prudential. Only two of nine proposed squares were finished, and proved so difficult to sell or rent that they were offered to army officers serving in Copenhagen rent free for the first year if the tenant agreed to install curtains. Today they are more popular, being ideal family homes.

With their clean, white stucco façades, steps up to front doors with glazed lights above, and multi-paned windows, the houses are a pleasing hybrid of Danish and English neoclassical style. Inside, there are parquet floors, high ceilings, panelled doors, and refined plaster mouldings. The flat, cool northern light pours through big windows, and a small garden with a white picket fence at the back

THIS PAGE Opposite the sofa in the reception room at the back of the house is a superbly elegant rosewood desk by Frits Henningsen dating from the first half of the 20th century. The painting to the left of the glass-fronted cabinet is by renowned Danish artist Kurt Trampedach, bought on impulse by Karina, who has always loved his work, as she was passing Galerie Bechman in Copenhagen.

opens into an area of lawns and neatly clipped trees. 'It is a wonderful place for the boys,' Karina comments. 'The beach is within walking distance, and there are children in the other houses in the square they can play with. Everyone's back door is open in the summer, and when you need to find your children, you look for their shoes left outside.'

As is typical of English town houses of this date, the lower-ground floor was originally the domain of servants. In Karina's house, the hard work of taking down the walls that once chopped it into hall, maid's room, pantry, scullery, and kitchen had already been done. There is a bedroom and bathroom for the au pair, and a utility room, but the rest is a single space big enough for a generous kitchen area and a table that seats ten, 'or a whole class of children, if they don't mind sitting two to a chair,' says Karina.

On the floor above are the two main receptions room, linked by double doors, and on the first floor are three large bedrooms, and a dressing room and bathroom, the latter a more recent addition, as the houses were designed without bathrooms. The boys' rooms are busy with Lego, models, maps, books, and computers, but elsewhere there is a calm, spare, almost minimalist feel. 'When I bought this house, which I loved the moment I stepped through the front door,

I decided that for the first time in my life I would not compromise on its interior design,' says Karina. 'I would have exactly what I wanted.'

Jannik Martensen-Larsen of Danish design company Tapet-Café helped with curtains, upholstery, encouragement, and advice. But the rest is Karina: the colour palette of shades of grey, the mix of refined antiques and mid-20th-century design, the combination of poise and comfort. Surprisingly, Karina's starting point for the interior turns out to be one of the boldest splashes of colour in the house, the Pierre Frey 'Ming' fabric in Fuchsia that she has used for the bedroom blinds and the bed hangings draped from a corona painted in 'Radicchio'. 'I love this fabric, and the blue Pierre Frey I have used for the blind in the front living room, and I really like grey flannel for upholstery,' she says. 'I also knew I wanted

ABOVE LEFT The bathroom with its curved roof, which reminds Karina of being in an old-fashioned railway carriage, was a later addition to a house that was built without one. The woodwork is 'Hardwick White' against walls of 'All White'.

ABOVE RIGHT Both Karina's sons love Lego, one of Denmark's most famous exports. A particularly complicated Lego creation is taking shape on the desk of Victor's bedroom, a room that is painted 'All White.'

the walls to be grey. I had used Farrow & Ball paints for my flat in London and particularly appreciate their depth of colour and the matt finish of the emulsion. Also, it was a huge advantage to have so many shades of grey to choose from.'

Karina has used three Farrow & Ball greys in the house, six if you count 'Hardwick White' for the bathroom, 'Off-Black' for the stair banister and a pair of side tables in the hall, and 'Pitch Black' for a bench in the kitchen. The bedroom is 'Down Pipe', the rear of the double living room is 'Manor House Gray', and the front is 'Plummett'. Contrasted with snowy 'All White' gloss for woodwork and emulsion on ceilings and other walls, the effect is as chic and timeless as a pinstripe suit with a crisp white shirt. And, just as the smart but sober city gent might add a flourish of colour with tie and handkerchief, Karina has piped her grey flannel upholstery with velvet in burnt orange and periwinkle blue, and piled the vintage-leather corner sofa with cushions in the same blue velvet.

Equally eye-catching are the bold juxtapositions of pictures and furnishings, and some arresting individual pieces. The wall above the leather sofa, for example, is covered with a close tessellation of frames of different sizes but identical design. Karina bought them in IKEA and is slowly filling them with photographs. A delicate tree made from coloured telephone wire sits on one of a pair of console tables in the hall beneath a bowler-hat light. Above its twin hangs an installation of light bulbs mounted on patinated metal, and beneath it an abstract marble sculpture by Andrzej Lemiszewski. It is highly individual, and exactly what Karina wanted.

OPPOSITE AND THIS PAGE The main bedroom, at the front of the house, is the only one to have the same parquet flooring as the reception rooms, as well as a corner stove, and plaster ceiling mouldings. The combination of dark mahogany antique furnishings, the crisp raspberry on white of the Pierre Frey fabric, and the dark grey 'Down Pipe' on the walls is sophisticated and as smart as a pinstripe suit with a starched white shirt and an old school tie.

THIS PAGE AND OPPOSITE
LEFT Mamuka Bliadze was
initially resistant to the idea of
strong colour for the walls, but
once converted he embraced
it fully and chose the Archive
colour 'Saxon Green' in the
study, seen here from the
entrance hall, as an ideal
background for a pair of
paintings by Bruce McLean.
Painted 'Dix Blue', the entrance
hall also contains important
artworks including a large oil
by Matthias Weischer and
a sculpture by Tony Cragg.

ART HOUSE

Walk through the front door of Mamuka Bliadze's first-floor Berlin apartment and you step into a world of colour. The walls are blue, the armchairs are fuchsia, the cushions are turquoise. Through arched double doors to the left, the kitchen is a vibrant terracotta, while a doorway ahead frames a view of green walls, an orange chair, a purple cushion, mustard-yellow sideboard, and, hanging above it, an oil painting by Bruce McLean in neon tangerine, azure, and lime.

ABOVE RIGHT The entrance hall once housed the main staircase before the building was divided into separate apartments and is big enough to feel like a room in its own right, with a wall of bookshelves opposite a monumental new fireplace in polished concrete. The oil painting, vibrant and unframed on its background of 'Dix Blue', is by Georgian artist Natela Iankoshvili.

ABOVE AND RIGHT There are two grandly proportioned reception rooms. This one overlooks the street, and in summer its view of the houses opposite is veiled by the canopy of trees that lines the pavement. The fluid colour of the light-dappled leaves is reflected inside by walls of gentle 'Saxon Green', against which Bruce McLean's painted flowers and foliage pulsate with neon. Back-to-back desks shelter beneath a Triennale lamp by Arredoluce.

Mamuka Bliadze is a dealer in contemporary art, and lives above the gallery he runs with partners Alfred Kornfeld and Anne Langmann, surrounded by the paintings, sculptures, and photographs he loves, collects, buys, and sells. When he first viewed the apartment with interior architects Gisbert Pöppler and Rüdiger Sander, his impression was not immediately favourable. 'It seemed very dark,' he grimaces. 'It was being used as office space and a lecture hall for a publisher. They had painted it all white, but the effect was somehow murky. Instead of making the rooms feel bright, the white paint emphasized the lack of natural light.'

What the apartment lacked in sunlight, it made up for in architectural stature. In a quiet road in central Berlin, the building dates from 1892 and was designed by architect Wilhelm Martens as a studio and home for himself. These first-floor rooms were the main reception rooms and have soaring ceilings, tall doors, and big windows. However, at both the front

and the back, the windows are shaded by mature trees. Add to this the depth of the building, which is part of a terrace, and it is inevitable that the gracious, elegant interiors are a little deprived of natural light.

Rüdiger, who took charge of the project, knew that the solution was to use colour, and the best artificial lighting, to warm the spaces and dispel any trace of gloom. Mamuka, however, was initially concerned that his paintings would not look at their best against coloured backgrounds. Plain white walls remain the accepted, acceptable choice for displaying contemporary artworks, a rule adhered to by most galleries and museums. The bold, enveloping colour that Rudiger prescribed to transform the rooms from gloom to glory was a departure about which Mamuka was initially cautious.

Fortunately, Mamuka is adventurous and visually confident – he has, after all, helped to propel to fame and fortune several artists from his native Georgia, including Tamara Kvesitadze who represented her country in the 2007 Venice Biennale. He is also a man who is prepared to listen to expert advice, so when Rüdiger suggested 'Charlotte's Locks', one of the most punchy colours in the Farrow & Ball range, for the kitchen and dining room, Mamuka agreed.

THIS PICTURE Shelving in 'All White' can be pulled across to divide the 'Saxon Green' study from the living room, the walls of which are a more sober 'Hardwick White'. Although the decoration of this second reception room is less colourful, the two rooms feel balanced due to the expanse of bright red upholstery and the midnight blue of the rug by Jan Kath. The painting above the chair is by Neo Rauch, while the one propped against the shelves is by Tamara Kvesitadze.

'Dix Blue' was chosen for the hall, 'Hardwick White' for the drawing room, and Bliadze himself, by this stage a convert to the power of bold backgrounds, suggested 'Saxon Green' for the study, in which he planned to hang his prized pair of paintings by Bruce McLean. The effect of these paintings, which pulse with colour like an exotic, Impressionist jungle, and the enveloping greenery of the walls give the room a fresh, outdoor feel.

In the hall, where a large, lush landscape featuring a caravan by Matthias Weischer hangs opposite the front door, the blue of the wall that surrounds it picks up on the colour of the sky and makes the room feel bright and summery. More colour magic has been woven in the cloakroom and shower, which are slotted into an awkward space off the hall, where the sandy brown tones of 'India Yellow' are transformed to bright buttercup thanks to their juxtaposition with shiny black mosaic tiling.

The bedroom has a more subdued colour scheme, although Rüdiger has again exploited the power of paint by using the darker 'Brassica' above dado level and 'Wimborne White' beneath, in order to make this small, square room with its high ceiling seem broader and less tall. 'Wimborne White' has also been used in the adjacent bathroom, which is lined

OPPOSITE Two sombre paintings by Anselm Kiefer hang in this room, their monochrome palette quietly complemented by the soft grey of the 'Hardwick White' walls. Behind the tousled chair by Franco Albini, a sculpture of a man by Tamara Kvesitadze tiptoes on butterflies towards the open door of the kitchen.

TOP To spread the visual weight of the Bulthaup kitchen units, the lower walls were panelled in blackened oak below the exuberant orange of 'Charlotte's Locks'. The Pathos table is by Antonio Citterio, the chairs by Warren Platner, and the 'cupboard' on the far wall is actually a delicate artwork by Tamara Kvesitadze.

ABOVE Looking across the living room from the entrance hall, a slice of another Anselm Kiefer painting is visible on the far wall. The sculpture behind the Eames lounger is a maquette for a larger piece by Tamara Kvesitadze.

with striking *striato nero* marble in bold stripes of black and white. 'We especially chose the marble to have as little yellow coloration as possible, which is very hard to find,' Rüdiger explains. 'The 'Wimborne White' has a warm tinge, which helped to make the marble look even whiter.'

Furnished with 20th- and 21st-century classics such as the Pathos dining table by Antonio Citterio, dining chairs by Warren Platner, a B&B Italia sofa, a coffee table by Charlotte Perriand, and rugs by Jan Kath, the apartment has immense aesthetic panache. But despite all this visual bounty, it is the art that most insistently draws the gaze, whether a neon light installation in the kitchen by Brigitte Cowan, a sinuous white sculpture of a man tiptoeing on butterflies by Tamara Kvesitadze, a desolate landscape encrusted with twigs by Anselm Kiefer, or a small, enigmatic oil by Neo Rauch. All demand attention and examination.

'The colour of these rooms makes me happy,' Mamuka grins. 'The paint is very subtle, very diverse; it changes according to the light.' He has even commissioned an in-situ artwork using Farrow & Ball paint, such is his faith in it. Inspired by their work in a Berlin restaurant, Mamuka asked artists Denis Vidinski and Patrick Voigt, known as 22quadrat, to produce something similar in the corner of his kitchen, using 'All White' Estate Emulsion on top of the background colour 'Charlotte's Locks'. The result is a series of broad, textured brush strokes that descend raggedly from the cornice and terminate in thin drizzles of paint as if abandoned by some particularly slapdash, if creative, decorator. Yet another work of art shown off to advantage.

ABOVE The bedroom at the back of the apartment is small, particularly in relation to its ceiling height. By painting the walls in warm but receding 'Brassica' above the dado level, the space is optically expanded. The large-scale design of the Dedar curtains also helps to make the room seem bigger.

RIGHT Seen next to a bright white, earthy 'India Yellow' looks more tan than buttercup, but in this small, slick shower room, where it sits side by side with glossy black mosaic tiling and marble, it takes on a rich, golden glow.

THIS PAGE Opening from the main bedroom is this ultra-glamorous bathroom, lined in two types of dramatically striped Italian marble, superbly matched and chosen with as little yellow in the stone as possible. The subtle warmth of 'Wimborne White' on the walls helps to make the marble seem whiter still. The column heaters are from Tubes Radiators.

DECORATING PRINCIPLE 3

Creative Inspiration

Paint and wallpaper can be addictive. You may start on the walls but find the habit extending to everything from the legs of the kitchen table to the covers of photograph albums. Be creative and you can get your fix of pattern by using wallpaper on boxes and lampshades or to line a glass-fronted cabinet or the back of shelves, and enjoy a satisfying extra helping of colour by painting the inside of cupboards or even a shaped headboard on the wall behind your bed.

OPPOSITE Far from a decorating blunder, these brush strokes in 'All White' over 'Charlotte's Locks' were commissioned from artists 22quadrat to make an original Farrow & Ball installation in the corner of Mamuka Bliadze's kitchen (see pages 52–61). While the effect might be a little too anarchic for most of us, a simple mural, stencil, or hand-painted stripe can add a personal feel to a room, even if you are only brave enough to try it in the cloakroom.

ABOVE RIGHT A less challenging Farrow & Ball artwork hangs in a bedroom of Eva Gnaedinger's house (see pages 96–103), consisting of two squares of painted board, one in 'Down Pipe', the other in 'Elephant's Breath', with a scrap of rough, unbleached linen at its centre. Without starting from scratch, you can transform the look of an existing picture by painting its frame in just the right shade.

RIGHT Painting the inside of shelves or cabinets is a good way to introduce a controlled dose of a new colour into a room. Here, 'Cinder Rose' draws the eye to the delicate and intriguing contents of the shelves in Jorge Almada and Anne-Marie Midy's Paris apartment (see pages 80–85).

THIS PAGE Most of the walls in the flat are painted in neutral colours that provide a calm, elegant setting for the paintings and antiques collected by Liz and David Smith. The drawing room is 'String', a warm, pale-earth pigment-based colour that picks up the marble of the Regency chimneypiece that is the focus of the room.

MOVING UP

Emma Burns and Liz Smith have known one another for a long time. Emma Burns is a seasoned and discreetly grand decorator, a director of Sibyl Colefax & John Fowler, one of the oldest and most revered of decorating firms. But when Liz Smith first met her, some 30 years ago, she was a humble assistant at another decorating firm, Charles Hammond, and still living with her parents. 'I went into the Charles Hammond shop to ask for a swatch of fabric,' Liz Smith remembers, 'and Emma said she would send it to me. When I wrote down my address, she realized we were neighbours and said she would pop it through the letterbox instead. She was charming and efficient.'

ABOVE Emma Burns's architectural adjustments to the entrance hall included moving a door so that the view from the front door is a charming composition of needlepoint chair and 18th-century engravings. Liz chose the large-scale 'St Antoine' wallpaper above a dado in 'Old White' and grounded it by using 'Railings' for the skirting/baseboard, a decorative device popular in Regency interiors.

Liz Smith and her late husband David became friends with Emma's parents, initially bonding over a mutual love of pugs. Meanwhile, Emma steadily worked her way from shop girl at Charles Hammond to manager for the Colefax & Fowler fabric showroom, through assistant to legendary decorator Roger Banks-Pye to running her own design team. When Emma took on her parents' house in a central London square and moved in with her two children, she became Liz Smith's neighbour for a second time. 'She completely transformed that house,' Liz Smith

enthuses. 'I remember going to see it and being amazed by how she had reorganized the space, and by the subtlety of the colours she used. It was very impressive. So when David suggested we should move from our house to a flat, I agreed – but only on the condition that we could employ Emma to help us with the interior design.'

Now semi-retired, Liz Smith has had an extremely successful career as a fashion journalist, working as Fashion Editor for various magazines and newspapers including the *Observer*, and *The Times*, writing, and styling shoots with photographers such as Norman Parkinson, Helmut Newton, and Sarah Moon. Her husband David Smith, a senior Creative Director, also worked in a world dominated by the visual. Add Emma into the mix and you have three experienced professionals, all with strong ideas of their own on taste and style, all working on the same project. The result might have been a clash, but instead was a creative and happy collaboration. 'Emma understood so perfectly how David and I lived, and is brilliant at juggling space. It was great to work with such a perfectionist,' Liz says.

The flat Liz and David decided to buy is on the third floor of a red-brick mansion block overlooking the trees of a garden square: quiet, convenient, smart. Inside, it was not quite so perfect. 'It had been messed around,' Emma recalls. 'Some of the proportions didn't feel right, and a lot of its original architectural detailing had been lost in the wash.' Emma set about restoring order and harmony; moving a door here, lowering a ceiling there, 'robbing Peter to pay Paul,' as she puts it, by shaving space off a dressing room to make a bigger guest bedroom. Back went cornices and skirtings/baseboards, and the drawing room was given the elegant focus of a particularly pretty Regency fireplace that Liz and David had found for the drawing room of their last house and brought with them.

Some of Emma's adjustments are so subtle that their effect is almost subliminal. In the drawing room, for example, there was an opening where it had been knocked through into the adjacent dining room to make a single, open-plan space. But the opening was too low and too narrow, and, according to Emma, felt 'mean'. Not only did she raise and widen the aperture itself, she also built floor-to-ceiling bookcases on the drawing-room side of the dividing wall, instantly tripling the depth of the opening and making it feel substantial. A similar architectural

ABOVE LEFT 'String' complements the antique marble chimneypiece that was bought for a previous house and now sets the aesthetic tone for Liz and David's drawing room.

BELOW LEFT Bookshelves surround the opening between the drawing room and dining room, adding crucial depth and architectural heft to this transition between the two spaces.

THIS PAGE David designed the book and television cabinet, which is painted 'Book Room Red' beneath a top of black Belgian fossil marble. The set of drawings above are of Emma Hamilton's 'Attitudes', a form of mime developed by Nelson's future mistress to portray classical figures such as Cleopatra and Cassandra.

ABOVE The flat had lost much of its architectural detailing, which Emma was at pains to restore, such as this door with its leaded glass above. She also reintroduced skirtings/baseboards and cornices.

sleight of hand transformed the entrance hall, where she shunted the cloakroom door facing the front door over to the left and built out a buttress of wall to mask it and to give the space a slightly more room-like feel.

No one would deny the importance of first impressions, and this entrance hall, once a non-event, has undoubtedly been improved by surgery, but it has been made all the more striking by the bold choice of the large-scale 'St Antoine' wallpaper in graphic charcoal 'Railings' on 'Old White'. The monochrome pattern covers the walls from dado rail to cornice, and is cleverly grounded by a dark strip of skirting, also in 'Railings', where the walls meet the floor. Liz is characteristically modest about her contributions to the design of the flat, but quietly admits that the wallpaper was her idea. 'Emma and I went to Farrow & Ball together, and had such fun choosing. We both love the colours.' Emma agrees. 'There is a wonderful range of colours, and they are all so reliable. You know you will get a good result.'

Elsewhere, they have chosen neutral shades as a backdrop to Liz and David's collection of paintings, prints, books, and furnishings. The kitchen is 'Hardwick White'. 'I adore it', says Liz. 'It's been up for seven years,' adds Emma, 'and it still looks immaculate.' A notable exception to the neutrals is the low bookcase and cupboard in the drawing room, designed by David to hide the television. It was Emma's decision to paint this 'Book Room Red'. 'The depth of this colour, and what I call the "dirt" in its make-up, means it reads as if it were a polished wood,' she explains. 'An experienced decorator can suggest colours that might seem frightening to a lay person.' Just one of the advantages of calling in a professional, as Liz Smith will attest. 'We didn't have the benefit of Emma's help in our last house,' she comments. 'Emma added real polish.'

TOP LEFT The small, square kitchen has a single window tucked into its corner, which Emma has made the most of by installing a fitted corner seat with a padded cushion over a radiator cover. The diminutive, folding coaching table is the perfect size for the space, and the set of children's alphabet illustrations, hung high enough not to interfere with the seating, adds an appealing note of levity.

ABOVE LEFT Tumbled marble mosaic tiling in the cloakroom is complemented by paintwork in 'Smoked Trout'. Here, the same paint colour has been used for the woodwork as for the walls, a decorating trick that makes a small space seem larger by minimizing contrast and unnecessary detail.

ABOVE Warm, grey 'Hardwick White' covers the walls, wall panelling, and cupboards in the kitchen. Specially made joinery makes use of every inch of space, and the combination of the paint colour with grey marble and brushed stainless steel is as practical as it is sophisticated.

DECORATING PRINCIPLE 4

Painted Furniture

Paint is visual magic, and the better quality the paint, the more powerful the spell. This is particularly apparent on furniture, when a perfect gloss or satiny eggshell can bestow gravity and charm on an otherwise nondescript chair or chest of drawers, providing a substitute for lack of patina, disguising cheap materials and unifying awkward mends, marriages, and bodges. It can also dignify all manner of designs in utilitarian MDF, from kitchen cabinets to faux-Georgian panelling.

RIGHT Decorator Emma Burns chose 'Book Room Red' for the shelves and television cupboard in this drawing room (see pages 64–69). 'The depth of the colour reads as if it were a polished wood,' she explains, 'and has enough "dirt" in its make-up. Visually, it supports the black Belgian fossil top, and is a warm addition to the scheme of the room.'

OPPOSITE ABOVE LEFT An old, planked door resting on low trestles makes a coffee table in Sophie Lambert's elegant drawing room (see pages 152–159). She has used 'Pigeon' in Estate Emulsion for a matt finish, which she has distressed with a very dilute solution of *bitume de judée*.

OPPOSITE BELOW LEFT Eva Gnaedinger (see pages 96–103) found this daybed on a skip/dumpster. She painted it 'Off-Black', and made a new mattress. Draped in sheepskins, it sits on her terrace overlooking Lake Maggiore.

OPPOSITE ABOVE RIGHT AND BELOW RIGHT Juliette Bartillat (see pages 132–141) has painted two items of furniture in a favourite shade, 'Railings'. In the kitchen, the colour smartens a set of shelves that stand out against walls in bright 'Blazer'. In a bedroom, where walls and woodwork are 'Dimity', an armoire is given a grand presence by a coat of the same dark colour.

CONTEMPORARY

The rooms on the following pages have almost all been created in old buildings, including a 17th-century canal house in Amsterdam, an 18th-century mansion in Paris, and a mid-20th-century neoclassical apartment block in Rome. Some retain period features, and some feature antique furnishings, but the way each interior has been put together gives them an unmistakably contemporary feel. All the colours and patterns chosen to create these effects are by Farrow & Ball.

ABOVE Walls in 'Light Gray'. **OPPOSITE** Left-hand wall in 'Cinder Rose', other walls
'Dimity' with a cupboard painted 'Churlish Green'.

DUTCH COURAGE

Matt pink with gloss black is not a paint scheme you would necessarily expect from a fashion-conscious interior decorator with a thing for motorbikes. Yet (aside from an entrance hall in dark 'Mahogany') 'Setting Plaster' and 'Pitch Black' are the two colours James van der Velden has chosen for the flat he shares with his girlfriend, Suzette van Dam. On the top floor of a 17th-century canal house in Amsterdam, the flat has sloping ceilings supported by hefty wooden beams. Rather than attempting to minimize the presence of these slabs of wood, James has given them even more heft by painting them gloss black, in stark contrast with the soft blush of the walls. 'The beams are such an amazing feature that I wanted to make the most of them,' he says, 'while the pink felt more in tune with the age of the building.'

The effect is surprisingly masculine and serves to highlight the structural engineering that underpins the elegant architecture of these tall, terraced houses. The building belongs to Suzette's brother, which is how she and James were lucky enough to find a home with such a prestigious address. It was built by architect Pieter Vingbooms and was originally offices and accommodation for high-ranking officials of the VOC, the Verenigde

OPPOSITE A small kitchen looks into the living room through a hatch above the pair of armchairs. The beams painted in glossy 'Pitch Black' run across the apartment from side to side and the walls are 'Setting Plaster'.

RIGHT This is the view through the kitchen hatch into the living room. The kitchen is painted in 'Mahogany', as is the windowless entrance hall. The very dark colour intensifies the sense of light and space in the rooms that open off the hall and have windows at the front and back of this tall, terraced house.

BELOW Items from James's collection are ranged on shelves, also painted 'Pitch Black', on either side of the wall-mounted flat-screen television.

Oost-Indische Compagnie or Dutch East India Company. On the first floor there is a ballroom once used for the 17th- and 18th-century equivalent of corporate entertaining. More recently, the building was a bank with a safe in the basement, so large and heavy it had to be lifted out by crane.

Getting things into James's flat on the sixth floor, with no lift and the only access via a steep, narrow staircase, was also a logistical problem. 'We did a complete remodelling, including putting in old wooden floorboards,' says James.

'Most problematic of all were the two motorbikes, which I wanted to park on a beam above the living room. We managed to get them through the front windows on a mobile lift,' he explains, 'but then we had to carry them up the ladder staircase to the mezzanine level under the roof, and put a plank across the beams so we could wheel them into place. I had asked a few friends to help out on the day we moved in, and they were not too happy to find themselves manhandling motorbikes in incredibly awkward spaces.'

OPPOSITE BELOW The rough wooden floorboards, with their robust, industrial feel, were installed by James as part of a major remodelling of this 350-year-old attic. The sturdy framework of beams and rafters that supports the steep, gabled roof is emphasized by the glossy 'Pitch Black' paint, while the 'Setting Plaster' of the walls has a more historic and domestic feel. The section of ceiling above the two front windows supports two Honda motorbikes, installed by James for decorative effect.

RIGHT Behind the sofa in the living room is a dining table, made to James's design from reclaimed beams braced and supported by heavy metal straps. The hatch window opens onto a view of the gable of the house next door. Ceilings and woodwork throughout are 'Cornforth White'.

BELOW A ladder staircase, also 'Pitch Black', and doubling as a bookshelf, rises to the mezzanine study tucked neatly under the pitch of the roof. The stuffed goose and turtle beneath are standing on the open pages of a book of photography by Helmut Newton.

James is a collector and says he is very bad at throwing things away. 'I love items that have a story, so I always buy things in flea markets, small antiques shops, and during my travels. The flat is slowly filling up, which sometimes aggravates Suzette, but it all means something to me, whether the collection of glass bottles I bought in Zanzibar, the slave bracelet we brought back from South Africa, or the antique camera on a tripod that I found in a street market and made into a lamp.'

James's collections are the most intriguing feature of the apartment, aside from the robust, semi-industrial feel of the architecture. Animals and parts of animals are a dominant theme; in the living room there are three stuffed turtles and a stuffed goose, deer skins laid over chairs, a rabbit-fur rug, several stuffed birds, ostrich eggs, a giant turtle shell, a horn beaker full of porcupine quills, the head of a baby crocodile, mounted antlers, a feather fan, and a large cowrie shell. In the entrance hall there are framed butterflies and beetles. Even in the bedroom there is a stuffed pheasant, as well as more deer skins and an African horsehair fly switch.

LEFT The study is James's space, with a view of two motorbikes resting on a section of ceiling above the living room. Here the scaffolding of old beams is painted 'Lamp Room Gray' against plaster in 'Cornforth White'. Unlike the gloss 'Pitch Black', this receding colour in eggshell serves to mitigate, rather than emphasize, their presence in a space that might otherwise have felt cramped. Skylights in the vertiginous roof make this a light and airy den.

OPPOSITE ABOVE The unusual palette of 'Pitch Black' gloss and 'Setting Plaster' emulsion is carried through in the bedroom furnishings, with a black ash chest of drawers supporting a large urn-shaped lamp and television, next to a mirror with a heavy black ash frame. The effect is softened by the natural colours and textures of coir matting and unbleached linen bedclothes.

OPPOSITE BELOW Looking across the bed, you can see straight through the dark 'Mahogany' entrance hall and into the living room beyond, where a collage of a nude figure hangs between the front windows.

There is something of the Edwardian museum, or 17th-century cabinet of curiosities, about this plunder from the natural world. The effect is intensified by the accompanying collection of glass domes that, instead of protecting intricate Victorian arrangements of wax flowers or spun glass galleons, rises over all manner of oddities, from the more conventional birds on a perch to a china dog skull sitting on two Penguin paperbacks, or just four light bulbs. Big glass jars serve a similar purpose, one holding a mass of twisting twigs, another more light bulbs.

Carefully arranged on deep shelves, or grouped on side tables, an old trunk, or a stack of leather suitcases, this forest of objects creates an effect that is fashionable rather than old-fashioned because of the way antique and vintage items are juxtaposed with the ultra modern, such as the giant flat-screen television that is mounted on the chimneybreast. Like the contrast between the matt pink walls and the sheen of the gloss black beams, there is a constant interplay between reclaimed materials and modern design, with antiques reused and re-presented, whether 19th-century paperback books tied up with string and posed as part of a tablescape, old wine boxes used for side tables, or the dining table made from reclaimed wooden beams locked together with industrial metal braces.

Having studied interior design in London, followed by an internship and a job with Kelly Hoppen, a couple of years ago James started his own interior design company, Bricks. 'The inspirations for my work are travel, markets, and my childhood home. I love looking at industrial spaces and old cabins, and I am always attracted to the aesthetic of vintage items such as cameras and typewriters. We have worked on everything from a single bathroom to the design of a hotel chain, but I try to create a story and a distinctive feel for each project.'

In his mezzanine study in the pitch of the roof, James indulges his passion for boys' toys. Here, with a view of his two treasured motorbikes parked over the living room, he keeps his electric guitar, his vinyl records, his cameras, Lego, toy robot, model cars, air rifle, clocks, pipe, and cigar box. Suzette's equivalent personal territory is the second bedroom, a glamorous walk-in wardrobe where she keeps the beautiful clothes that are her own passion, and have become her career as founder of online fashion boutique thecollector.com. Fortunately for domestic harmony, it seems collecting is a shared enthusiasm.

A SHIPSHAPE HOME

In the middle of Paris, on a discreet side street close to Place des Vosges, Notre Dame, and the Louvre, in the attic of a grand 18th-century hôtel particulier, Jorge Almada and Anne-Marie Midy have found their ideal pied-à-terre. 'It's a dream,' Jorge enthuses. 'Because of the large paved courtyard in front of the building, and the immense garden at the side, there is a noise buffer which means the apartment is very quiet. Being up under the slope of the roof, with exposed beams and small windows on either side of the main room, makes it feel like living in the inverted hull of an old ship – something our boys love to imagine.'

ABOVE LEFT AND RIGHT In the entrance hall, the wall opposite the windows is 'London Clay', a warm, dark brown that has been used throughout the apartment. The apartment is so bright, with windows on all sides and also skylights, that the dark colour seems to reflect rather than absorb light, while acting as a superb background to objects as diverse as this painted terracotta urn and rough wooden picture.

LEFT Curtains are looped back on either side of the entrance to the main room from the hall. Walls are 'All White' except for the far wall, which is again 'London Clay'.

OPPOSITE Opening from the main room is a door onto a balustraded balcony with a view across the walled garden of this Parisian mansion and beyond over the roof-tops of central Paris. The sofa, armchairs, coffee table, and dining table are all by Casamidy.

Jorge and Anne-Marie are a cosmopolitan pair: Jorge is Mexican, while Anne-Marie is French and spent her childhood in Paris and visiting her grandparents' house in the South of France, a house that she is currently renovating. They met in America, where they were both studying design, and when they married they moved to the small Mexican hill-town of San Miguel de Allende, attracted by its colonial beauty and its thriving community of traditional craftsmen working with metal, leather, wood, and glass. This is where their furniture-making business, Casamidy, was born, and this is where its products are made, by local

craftsmen in small workshops, from where they are shipped all over the world: curvy metal chairs with sturdy leather seats, chunky wooden sofas upholstered in heavy-duty canvas, and mirrors with ornate frames of sculpted wrought iron or hammered tin.

After ten years in San Miguel, Jorge and Anne-Marie moved to Brussels with their two young sons. Brussels is their family home, San Miguel their business home, but the Paris apartment is rarely empty. They often visit for long weekends, and also rent it out on a weekly basis to Casamidy clients who, Jorge says, 'really appreciate the details Anne-Marie has created'.

It is hard to imagine a more inspiring architectural environment. Built as a private mansion for Franz-Joseph d'Hallwyl between 1766 and 1770 by the renowned neoclassical architect Claude Nicolas Ledoux, the stables of the Hôtel d'Hallwyl were big enough to accommodate 18 horses. For many years now it has been divided into separate apartments. Those on the ground and first floors have appropriately grand proportions, but Anne-Marie and Jorge's space was once the domain of servants. The journey from the street to their inner front door is an aesthetic delight, through the massive street entrance that towers over the narrow pavement like the wooden gates of a Roman

OPPOSITE ABOVE The 'London Clay' of the end wall not only serves to outline the interesting inverted boat shape of the roof line, it also frames a poised composition of sofa, armchairs, and pictures, acting as a strong focus in a room with no fireplace or other obvious focal point. The geometry of the neatly ranked cushions and the flat-weave rug are subtly complementary.

OPPOSITE BELOW Looking back in the other direction, the kitchen can be glimpsed through a hatch. The dining table with its patinated copper top is by Casamidy, but the wooden benches are antique.

ABOVE Set into the sloping eaves on either side of the room, the interior of these shelves is painted in 'Cinder Rose', picking up on the hue of the cushions on the sofa, and giving added depth to a space where precious objects are displayed, here a jade elephant, a miniature oriental screen, and a trio of dried roses.

RIGHT Novel use has been made of an old artist's easel as an adjustable stand for the flat-screen television.

palace, to the symmetrical, classical beauty of the courtyard within, to the wide sweep of the stone staircase with its graceful metal balustrade, and up a final flight of wooden stairs to the top.

Although the rooms on this floor were originally humble and hidden, the space is surprisingly impressive. An entrance hall with a small bedroom and galley kitchen leading off to the left acts as prologue to the main room, which is entered through a pair of looped-back curtains. Walking through them you find yourself in a room that spans the building from side to side, reaches up into the pitch of the roof, and is lit by four dormer windows, one French door, and three skylights. Huge, white-washed beams support the pitch of the roof and the feel of the space is more country barn than neoclassical urban palace. The views from the balcony and from all the windows, however, could not be more urban: a tangle of roofs with rows

of pointy, zinc-clad gables, regiments of terracotta chimney pots, and to the south the fat blue pipes and red tanks of the top of the Pompidou Centre.

The far wall of this combined living room, dining room, and study is painted in 'London Clay' and the recesses of the low shelves set into the slope of the walls are smoky pink 'Cinder Rose'. 'London Clay' appears again in a cloakroom where it is used to dado level with white walls above, the edge marked by a wide strip of braid attached to the wall with decorative upholstery nails. As designers working with patinated metals, leather, and wood, Jorge and Anne-Marie have a heightened sensitivity to how colour can be used to complement and enhance natural materials, so the sandstone exterior of the building, which is still the colour of pale honey on the elevations protected from street pollution, was a starting point for their choice. 'London Clay' is an

LADIES
KINDLY DO YOUR
SOLICITING DISCREETLY

OPPOSITE ABOVE LEFT An ostentatiously ornate carved, painted, and gilded bedhead bought in Venice by Anne-Marie's French grandmother curves over the bed, outlined against the 'All White' of the walls.

OPPOSITE ABOVE RIGHT The wall opposite the bed is painted 'London Clay', forming a sharp line where it meets the 'All White' of the rest of the walls and sloping ceiling. A Casamidy metal chair stands beside the antique papier-mâché sewing table, and a Casamidy mirror hangs above the early 19th-century chest of drawers.

exceptional colour,' Jorge comments 'and changes with the light throughout the day in a spectrum of purples and browns. 'Cinder Rose' adds an additional interplay of colour, and we considered very carefully which walls were to be painted a colour and which left white because of the lack of symmetry and the irregularity of the interior.'

Beyond the main room is a second bedroom, also beamed and with a wall of 'London Clay' opposite the bed, again offsetting the white. But while the main room is almost exclusively furnished with pieces by Casamidy – including the chunky dining table with its top of patinated copper, the wide sofa upholstered in the same waxed cotton used to cover the backs of trucks in Mexico, and neat little upholstered radiator screens – here there are more antiques. The elaborate carved bedhead was bought in Venice by Anne-Marie's grandmother, and there are two elegant chests of drawers and a Victorian inlaid papier-mâché and mother-of-pearl work table. Like their own designs, the furnishings of the apartment bring together influences from France and from Mexico, as well as from different eras.

Anne-Marie and Jorge work separately on the Casamidy collection; Jorge's pieces tend to have a workmanlike feel, while Anne-Marie's are more obviously decorative, even whimsical. Their styles are nonetheless entirely complementary, the friction between the two adding the energy of contrast, not unlike that between the pristine 'All White' and the accent walls of dusky 'London Clay' in their lofty Parisian eyrie.

OPPOSITE BELOW LEFT At the foot of the bed, another handsome antique chest with a marble top supports candles decorated with fragile wax flowers. Against the wall in 'London Clay', the gilded frame of the early 19th-century portrait glints as it catches the light. A dark, receding background colour can make a painting come alive and seem to project itself into a room.

OPPOSITE BELOW RIGHT, AND ABOVE A door in the wall of the bedroom that is painted in 'London Clay' opens into a bathroom, which continues the contrast between dark and light with its walls in 'All White' and dark shelves and mirror frames. On the bed, the dusky velvet cushions and sombre stripes of the bedcover provide a visual counterweight to the colour of the wall opposite.

THIS PAGE At the back of the deep space that is the ground-floor kitchen, living room, and dining room, light drops through a first-floor light well onto a wall of roughly mortared masonry and a smooth, plastered wall painted in 'Shaded White'. Furnishings include a factory barrow and an 18th-century gilded bergère.

INDUSTRIAL AND CHIC

Laure Vial du Chatenet and her husband have made a home for themselves and their three children that is a triumph of style over content. Located in a newly fashionable area of Paris and set behind a narrow street of tall buildings, on the far side of a courtyard, the house was originally a fur factory and was later converted into offices. Hemmed in by tall blocks, its main source of natural light is from windows onto the courtyard. Upstairs rooms at the back are lit by a deep light well and the sparse daylight afforded by a few windows close to adjacent buildings. When Laure and Bertrand first viewed the space, there was dark fabric on the interior walls and not a single attractive architectural feature to fire the imagination.

The appeal was square footage and location. Armed with confidence and the professional help of their architect and friend Philippe Robert, Laure and Bertrand bought the building and set about seeking planning permission to transform this gloomy burrow of offices into a place they could enjoy inhabiting. The finished house is spacious, comfortable, and surprising. The gloom has been banished by maximizing every photon of daylight and supplementing it where necessary with artificial light

ABOVE The front wall of the ground floor is all window, frosted to just above head height for the sake of privacy, looking onto a courtyard set back from the street and surrounded by offices and flats. The curving chimney flue that hugs the central brick pillar is painted in 'Railings'.

BELOW A wall in Laure's first-floor office is painted 'Black Blue' and hung with framed images adapted from 18th-century prints and engravings for her interiors and homewares business, Maison Caumont.

ABOVE The shiny stainless steel of kitchen appliances and shelf supports have a workmanlike chic against the old brick walls. The wall and door to the right are 'Shaded White'. A cured ham in a stand sits on the top shelf.

that mimics its quality. Cunningly placed and angled mirrors reflect light, and there are no curtains to impede its flow through windows, both external and internal. A glazed rectangle in the ceiling allows light into the rear of the living room from the first-floor light well, and a large square of glass set into the floor at the front of the living room admits it into the television room in the basement below.

By peeling away ceiling, wall, and floor coverings, they have revealed structures and surfaces that give the space the architectural character it was lacking. Freed from its office partitions, the deep ground-floor room, fronted by a wall of windows onto the courtyard, is kitchen, dining room, and living room combined. Helping to divide the space into separate areas are a neat spiral staircase and a central column of brick hugged by a metal chimney flue. Some walls are bare brick, some smooth plaster. The back wall is roughly mortared stone and the ceiling above the kitchen is pitted concrete striped with old metal girders. Floorboards are painted in 'Shaded White'.

ABOVE LEFT Looking towards the back of the ground-floor living space, the central kitchen counter is to the left and the rear wall of mortared stonework is hung with Laure's collection of 18th-century portraits, which include images of her own ancestors. The large Indian horse was bought on impulse by Bertrand. Floorboards are 'Shaded White'.

ABOVE RIGHT An 18th-century gilded chair, covered in fabric by Maison Caumont, sits on the landing in front of fitted cupboards painted 'Off-Black'.

OPPOSITE The dining table, surrounded by Eames DSW chairs, stands in front of a cupboard made from a reclaimed door. Areas of plastered wall in 'Shaded White' alternate with areas of bare brick or stonework throughout the house, providing contrast and acting as a reminder of its industrial origins.

Into this semi-industrial space, Laure and Bertrand have introduced furnishings that are as diverse as the textures of the interior architecture. The seating includes two contemporary sofas, an 18th-century gilded bergère, a mid-century modern buttoned lounger and stool, and a set of Eames DSW dining chairs. There is an old wooden trolley that serves as a coffee table, and a rusting metal sideboard that holds, among other things, a fabric skeleton under a glass dome, an elaborately carved mirror, and a bright orange glass vase.

Most unexpected of all are the 18th-century portraits that Laure collects: pastels and oils in gilded and ebonized frames depicting women in powdered wigs and men with lace cuffs. These are grouped on the end wall next to the kitchen, the same wall against which stands a carved and painted Indian horse the size of a small pony. The contrasts between the polite polish of the portraits and the rugged, workmanlike wall they hang on, and between the Western faces and frills and the stylized elegance of the Asian horse, give the paintings a freshness and vitality that invites you to look at them with more attention than if they were hung in a drawing room furnished with antiques.

OPPOSITE The seating area at the front of the ground floor is the lightest part of the room adjacent to the front wall of floor-to-ceiling windows and here the 'Shaded White' of the walls is divided by a painted dado in 'Railings'. The old-fashioned column radiator is also 'Railings', its sculptural qualities on show against a background of 'Shaded White'. A square aperture in the floor beneath the vintage leather lounger is glazed in order to allow light into the television room in the basement below. The cushion is by Maison Caumont.

LEFT Laure's teenage daughter Marie has a bedroom painted 'Elephant's Breath' and a large collection of bags. As downstairs, the floor is 'Shaded White'.

ABOVE The spiral staircase from the ground floor leads up to a large landing area that gains light from a window onto the courtyard at the front of the building, and from a deep, glassed-in light well just to the right of this image, planted with ferns that give a green, aqueous cast to the light falling on walls and floor painted in 'Shaded White'.

Laure delights in 18th-century elegance, but also in a more contemporary taste for things that are frayed, rusted, and utilitarian, and it is the rub between the two that characterizes the style of her interiors company, Maison Caumont. From her shop in Montmartre, she sells fabrics, wallpapers, lamps and lampshades, pictures, cushions, stationery, and decorative objects, which adapt and subvert 18th-century prints and engravings, whether the poised head of a famous beauty or a study of a beetle.

Bertrand's business is shipping art and antiques, while Laure trained in art history and worked for an auction house before launching Maison Caumont. Laure's particular skill is in taking the past and transforming it to make something fresh and with a contemporary edge, and both she and Bertrand have an eye for the unusual and for a bargain. Bertrand bought the Indian horse on impulse at an auction where it was about to sell for a particularly low price. 'It has followed us everywhere ever since,' laughs Laure. In this house, it has been joined by a life-size sheep wearing a bowler hat and smoking a pipe, and a mouse dressed as a Degas ballerina, both by contemporary artist Mélanie Bourlon, whose work appeals to Laure's whimsical side.

Painted surfaces throughout the house are in Farrow & Ball, as are some pieces of furniture. 'For me, it is the best – very chic, very contemporary,' says Laure. 'If you look in the French decorating magazines you will see it used in all the smartest houses. All my friends use it. It's easy. I know the colours, and I know I love them.'

ABOVE LEFT Inserted into the main bedroom is a trapezoid-shaped bathroom with a window for borrowed light set in partition walls painted 'Shaded White'.

BELOW LEFT César's bedroom has a collection of vintage pedal cars parked on the wall. His bed is painted 'Off-Black' and the wardrobe on the left is 'Oval Room Blue'.

OPPOSITE A papier-mâché sculpture of a life-size mouse ballerina by Mélanie Bourlon, who also made the pipe-smoking sheep in the window of the living room, guards the door to Marie's bedroom, standing against walls of 'Shaded White'.

DECORATING PRINCIPLE 5

Painted Floors

Just as a coat of paint can revamp a piece of furniture, so it can conjure a completely new floor. Hard-wearing and practical, floor paint is perhaps the least-expensive way to ground a room, to enliven concrete, unify patched floorboards, or dignify hardboard. Whether wall-to-wall colour, a chequerboard design in imitation of tiles or stone, or a more complex pattern using stencils, the choice is as varied as if you were using carpet or rugs.

ABOVE RIGHT The staircase in this Norwegian cabin (see pages 144–151) has been given added visual interest with three different paint colours; 'Lamp Room Gray' for the treads, 'Dead Salmon' for the risers and banisters, and 'Mahogany' for the rail.

BELOW RIGHT Maud Steengracht has used 'Radicchio' to paint the floorboards in her kitchen (see pages 126–131). A dark colour gives a floor a sense of solidity and this type of red, with its tones of magenta and brown, has the traditional feel of terracotta tiles or polished brick.

CENTRE In a house almost entirely decorated in shades of white and off-white, including floorboards painted 'Old White', the vivid 'Eating Room Red' of the stairs that lead to Sophie Lambert's teenage son's bedroom (see pages 152–159) make a bold decorative statement.

OPPOSITE ABOVE RIGHT The concrete floor in Maud Steengracht's studio is painted 'Etruscan Red' and the ladder, which leads to storage in the roof, is in 'Ball Green' Floor Paint, chosen to minimize scuffing on its wooden treads. The warm red reflects a comforting glow in a room that might otherwise feel cold.

OPPOSITE BELOW RIGHT On the landing of Laure Vial du Chatenet's house (see pages 86–93), floorboards in 'Shaded White' maximize light.

NEUTRAL TERRITORY

Interior and lighting designer Eva Gnaedinger says she has only three criteria when it comes to buying a house: the location, the price, and enough space for a workshop. Eva's current home ticks the location box with a major flourish. Just over the Italian border at the Swiss end of Lake Maggiore, it is reached by a narrow road that zigzags up from the shore to a point from which the view is at its most spectacular. Even on a grey day, the lake glitters below, marbled by the breezes that brush its surface. On the far side, dark, wooded hills are sprinkled along their lower edges with the pink and white of distant houses that seem to have slipped down to gather near the water.

LEFT All that remains of the walls that once divided this impressive space is a supporting girder, which Eva has wrapped in a sleeve of linen. Walls and ceiling are 'Shaded White', grounded by flooring of slate-grey ceramic tiles. In this soothing medley of white, cream, and shades of brown, the textures of fur and sheepskin add visual interest as well as comfort.

RIGHT The tiled mosaic side of Eva's bathtub seen from the entrance hall with walls painted 'Shaded White'.

It took Eva five months of intensive searching to find this lakeside perch. 'So many of the houses round here have been overdone,' she says. 'People have spent a fortune on them – lining them with marble and filling them with designer furniture. This house was very ugly when I bought it. It hadn't been touched since it was built in the 1970s. The colours inside were horrible and the garden was full of orange, yellow, and red flowers. But the house itself doesn't matter, and neither does the colour of the flowers. You can change a house, and you can plant different flowers.'

In the few years since buying the house, Eva has done both these things, and so successfully that what the house lacks in architectural merit is forgotten in the lush, rambling charm of its surrounding garden and the chic, sophisticated comfort of its interiors. Because it is built on a hill, the garden and the house are on two levels. The upper level, which has a lawn and fruit trees at the side and a terrace at the front, is where Eva lives. The lower level, from which views of the lake are screened by surrounding trees and protective hedges, is a

OPPOSITE The wall that partially divides the living room from the kitchen also contains the flue of the fireplace. Above and to the left of the fireplace is another square aperture into which is set a flat-screen television. This wall is painted in 'Off-Black' so that the glow of the fire and the flicker of the television are thrown into bright relief against it. The sofa is from IKEA, the standard lamp was found in a thrift store and refurbished by Eva, and the stool was rescued from a skip/dumpster.

ABOVE Bright white kitchen units are set against walls of 'Light Gray'. The birds in a dome and fish in a glass case add unexpectedly decorative elements to an otherwise minimal scheme of clean-lined modernity.

RIGHT A wall of cupboards in 'Shaded White' and shelves screened by linen curtaining lead out from the kitchen to the upper lawn, with its fruit trees and hammock.

LEFT Sliding glass doors open from the living room onto a terrace with views of Lake Maggiore. The daybed is one of Eva's finds, and had been left out as rubbish. She painted it 'Off-Black'. The exterior walls are 'Mouse's Back' and the exterior woodwork is 'Shaded White'.

BELOW Eva's bedroom has a small balcony with one of the best views across the lake. Walls are 'Light Gray', as in the kitchen, but here the dusky mauve of bedlinen and curtains seems to bring out a hint of smoky green in this extremely subtle neutral, which can look more brown or grey according to the light.

OPPOSITE On the wall next to the Saarinen-style 1970s dining table, a pair of lamps and a vase of hydrangeas pick up on the blues of a painting by Kiddy Citny, the only deviation from a palette of coffee and cream in the rest of the room. The cupboards are 'Pointing' and this wall of the living room is 'Light Gray'.

separate one-bedroom apartment with its own kitchen and bathroom, and this Eva uses for guests or sometimes as rental accommodation. Next to it is her workshop, quite separate from her own living quarters but only requiring a commute from home to work down a couple of flights of garden steps. Here she designs, restores, and revamps a forest of lamps and chandeliers, and works on her interior design projects, currently a new hotel called Villa Orselina in nearby Locarno.

Unlike so many of her neighbours, Eva does not like to lavish unnecessary expense on a house. Her previous two houses, both in France, required careful restoration but already had beautiful bones: 'All you had to do to make a fabulous interior was clean the floor and put a candle on the mantelpiece.' Here, the design required more ingenuity. Nonetheless, Eva kept and reused as much as she could, including all the doors and windows. Her biggest bills came from knocking down internal walls to open the hall, kitchen, and living room into one big space, and to minimize the division between her bedroom and bathroom. The living-room ceiling already extended up into the pitch of the sloping roof – one of the things that first appealed to Eva about the house – but now the walls that chopped it into smaller spaces have gone, and the sense of volume is impressive.

Aside from the internal demolition, the installation of slate-grey ceramic floor tiles throughout, a pristine white kitchen, and new bathroom fittings, Eva says she has spent very little. She has even kept some of the original cupboards, repositioned and rejuvenated with paint and new handles. 'Most of the furnishings are from IKEA or thrift stores,' she

says proudly, 'and some of my best things I found in the garbage.' Instances of the latter include the daybed on the terrace, which she painted and made a mattress for, a stool by the fireplace that she also painted and reupholstered, and, most surprising of all, a gorgeous Barovier & Toso glass lamp that hangs in pride of place over the living-room sofas. Vintage lamps in Murano glass by Barovier & Toso are highly sought after and extremely expensive, so this was a particularly brilliant find.

The effect of all this thrift is remarkably luxurious. The straight-edged IKEA sofa is softened with sheepskin rugs and mounds of cushions covered in unbleached linen. More creamy sheepskins cloak the seats and backs of the modernist dining chair and the leather recliner, and a rabbit-skin rug provides a downy oasis on the cool floor tiles. Furnishings are clean white, sharp black, and any number of browns between the two; paint colours are neutral, natural, earth, and shadow: 'Light Gray', 'Shaded White', 'Stony Ground', 'Mouse's Back', 'Mahogany', and 'Off-Black'.

'I love colour,' Eva insists, 'but there is so much colour – you, me, flowers – that I like to create a calm background for it.'

Eva is devoted to Farrow & Ball paint. 'I first came across it when I was working on a house in France for some Americans. At first I thought they were extravagant, but I soon changed my mind and realized that this paint is worth the price. A friend who visited recently from New Zealand instantly noticed the special quality of the paint colours here. "They are so tactile," she said. "I just want to lie on them." And I knew exactly what she meant. They have a softness and a depth that you can't copy.'

Eva's devotion to Farrow & Ball extends to using it to create home-grown artworks. In the guest bedroom, against a wall painted 'Off-Black', hangs an intriguing painting. A close inspection reveals it to be a square of wood painted in 'Elephant's Breath' with a frayed square of natural linen glued onto it, mounted on a larger piece of wood that is painted in 'Down Pipe'. Like so many of Eva's inventions, it is highly effective. And like some of her most prized possessions, it cost virtually nothing.

OPPOSITE ABOVE This guest bedroom is an object lesson in how to create a striking interior with minimal outlay. The bed is from IKEA, the curtains are unlined linen scrim, and the artwork was made by Eva from a scrap of unbleached linen mounted on two pieces of board painted in 'Down Pipe' and 'Elephant's Breath'. This picture and the simple furnishings look striking and expensive against the dark background of the wall in 'Off-Black'.

OPPOSITE BELOW The guest shower room in the main house is painted in 'Mouse's Back', the same colour Eva has used for the exterior walls of the house.

THIS PAGE Opposite the shower room is a guest bedroom with walls painted in 'Stony Ground'. The luxurious feel of the purple velvet cushions is accentuated by the quiet modesty of the colours around them.

NEW LININGS

Marco Lobina, Isabella Errani, and their daughter Virginia used to live in an open-plan, minimalist loft with white walls. Marco runs a successful business from Turin selling 'rezina', a hard-wearing resin finish for walls and floors, a version of which can also be used as a sealant for waterproofing wallpaper and even fabrics. More recently, he has become a stockist for Farrow & Ball. Isabella is a high-powered PR based in Milan who represents top brands from Swarovski and Intimissimi to Wrangler and Fred Perry.

OPPOSITE The entrance hall walls and ceiling are lined with 'Tented Stripe' ST1366, outlined by skirtings/baseboards, woodwork, and cornice in 'Strong White'. Countering the traditional feel of a high-quality paper in a classic design are the resin floor, the Split bookcase by Peter Marigold, and the lurex fleck in the upholstery of the sofa.

TOP LEFT A detail of the panel over the 'Ranelagh' BP1823 wallpaper in the study.

ABOVE LEFT At the end of the central corridor, the door to a bedroom is glass, frosted in a perfect copy of the wallpaper stripe and reflected in the glossy resin flooring.

ABOVE RIGHT The apartment is on the first floor and the tall window of the study looks out on the leaves of a tree in front of the building. The plastered panels that partially obscure the wallpaper are painted 'All White'.

ABOVE LEFT The parquet flooring in the living room is made from wood reclaimed from an old boat and partially blackened by contact with salt water, hence the attractive two-tone effect. The wallpaper in this room is 'Melrose' BP1420, and the original casement windows, skirtings, and cornice are all 'Strong White'. The plaster panels are 'All White'.

ABOVE RIGHT Glazed doors lead from the living room to the dining room and from the dining room to the large roof terrace that first persuaded Marco and Isabella to buy the apartment. Surrounded by trellis covered in scented climbing plants, this is a private outdoor space in the middle of a city.

Both Marco and Isabella are acutely fashion conscious, embracing contemporary style with typically Italian confidence and enthusiasm. So it was initially a surprise to their friends and family when this thoroughly modern pair moved out of their loft and into an apartment, which they decorated with richly coloured, boldly patterned traditional English wallpaper.

'We had to move,' explains Marco. 'Virginia was 12 years old and it was becoming impossible to live in a space without separate rooms. We searched for many months and at last we found this, and it seemed perfect.' 'This' is a large, high-ceilinged apartment on the first floor of a 1940s block just off one of the main piazzas in the centre of Turin. The airy proportions and tall windows were part of the attraction, but the clincher was the roof terrace, larger than many urban gardens, overlooked by a gorgeously crumbling classical terrace of picturesque, rusting balconies and broken shutters, and with a view of the iconic tapering steeple known as La Mole Antonelliana, architectural symbol of the city of Turin.

Even if you had not known Marco and Isabella's previous apartment, you might find yourself surprised by their current one. The moment the heavy wooden front door swings open onto the entrance hall you are confronted by the unexpected. A wall of boldly striped wallpaper faces you, dark green on a buff background, matt, good quality, redolent of Regency splendour, expensive hotels, or exclusive London clubs. But this flourish of

THIS PAGE Like a giant open book with blank, white pages, plaster panels cover a corner of the dining room, which is papered on both walls and ceiling in 'Ivy' BP652. The chairs are Eames DSW, the chandelier is Lightweight by Tom Dixon, and the table in the corner is a design by Gio Ponti.

tradition is instantly undermined by contradictory and equally powerful visual signals. The floor is shiny, off-black, and glossy as a crow, and the stripy wallpaper, which also strides across the ceiling, is not continuous. The wall beside the front door is virginal, flat white, and is interrupted by two flush panels of heavily textured wood planking. Other areas of wall are partially obscured by white panels superimposed over the wallpaper.

Leading off the hall is a study, wallpapered in a punchy red and buff pattern with a distinctly Victorian gothic feel. A long corridor leads off the hall at right angles; along it, panelled double doors open onto Virginia's bedroom, which is papered in a terracotta stripe, the main bedroom, papered in broad stripes of dark and paler green, and the living room, with a bold flower pattern of cream on a pillar box-red background. The dining room sports a more subdued

BELOW The kitchen is the only room without wallpaper and is painted in Dead Flat 'Strong White', which gives a perfect, matt finish but is not normally recommended for kitchens and bathrooms because, in comparison with other finishes, it marks quite easily. Here, however, it remains immaculate and elegant, a setting for the sleek stainless steel sink and hob/stovetop by Arclinea and cupboards made from reclaimed French oak.

RIGHT A view through the door of the dining room with its asymmetrical frame of plaster panelling, across the central corridor and into the kitchen where a Camouflage lamp by Front Design is suspended over the stainless steel island that contains the sink. The wallpaper in the corridor is a continuation of the 'Tented Stripe' ST1366 in the entrance hall, the plaster panel is 'All White' Estate Emusion, and the woodwork is Estate Eggshell 'Strong White'. The Crisis dining table is by Piet Hein Eek.

design of green ivy leaves. Behind another door are golden bees on the walls of a shower room, while the bathroom adjoining the main bedroom is lined with a small repeat of spots, the sort of design you might find in the attic of an English country house.

All the wallpapers are by Farrow & Ball, in designs and colours at the more traditional end of the range. However, the way they have been used is so far from traditional that it verges on the revolutionary. The white panels are a feature of every room in the apartment, and cover walls in unexpected places; sometimes from floor to ceiling, sometimes from dado level to ceiling, sometimes continuing around windows and doors. They are made from aluminium panels filled with plaster, stand precisely 5cm/2in proud of the walls, and are bevelled to leave shadow-gaps, some of which are illuminated by strips of hidden lighting. The effect is as if fragments of a sleek, white minimalist loft apartment have been carefully inserted inside the architecture of an older building.

THIS PAGE Marco and Isabella's daughter Virginia's bedroom has been given exactly the same decorative treatment as the rest of the apartment, with plaster panels in 'All White' over 'Tented Stripe' ST1351 wallpaper. The sophistication of the scheme and the furnishings is barely compromised by a collection of aesthetically pleasing soft toys.

OPPOSITE ABOVE AND BELOW RIGHT The master bathroom is lined with 'Polka Square' BP1056 wallpaper that has been waterproofed with a resin finish developed by Marco's company Rezina, rendering it durable enough to be used inside a shower. The simple, geometric design works as well with the uncompromising modernity of the fittings as it would in an old-fashioned attic bedroom.

The clash is initially disconcerting – like seeing the Queen in platform shoes, or Prince Philip wearing a leather jacket – but it has been so beautifully done, with such care, precision, and craftsmanship, that it feels structural and permanent rather than insubstantial and pretentious. The idea was inspired when Marco and Isabella decided they did not want to erase the apartment's former splendour. 'It had been lived in by a Marchesa,' Marco explains, 'and the décor was grand and old-fashioned. We worked with Turin architects UdA (Ufficio di Architettura) to try to create a dialogue between that bourgeois opulence and our very modern sensibilities.'

This might all be a bit high falutin' were it not served up with such wit and panache. The visual joke of minimalist walls over lush wallpapers is echoed by stylistic quips and juxtapositions: a door panelled in mirror with frosted stripes that exactly match the painted stripes surrounding it; roughly planked kitchen cupboard doors that open to reveal slick, modern innards; and a selection of iconic and sometimes jokey modern furnishings, including the huge moon of a Camouflage lamp by Front Design suspended over the kitchen sink. Even the 19th-century buttoned sofa in the hall has been updated, thanks to its upholstery of grey linen flecked with a subtle gold lurex thread.

Marco was so inspired by the wallpapers that he arranged to open a Farrow & Ball showroom in Turin. On a quietly stylish side street, the shop is announced by an arcaded entrance that is lined with wallpaper. The arcade can be closed off from the pavement by metal shutters, but when they are open it is as if someone has decided to wallpaper the outside as well as the inside of the building, an effect almost as surprising as Marco's apartment.

ABOVE All the main rooms are grandly proportioned and the study, living room, and this main bedroom are entered through generous double doors painted 'Strong White' eggshell. In a less lofty space, the use of a dark wallpaper on the ceiling could induce a sense of claustrophia, but here the rich, forest greens of 'Broad Stripe' ST1330 striding overhead have no such effect, although like the décor in the rest of the apartment they are

visually surprising. Again, white panels fold around part of the room. The black standard lamp silhouetted against one of them in the corner is Fold by Established & Sons.

OPPOSITE BELOW LEFT The shower room across the corridor from Virginia's bedroom contrasts glamorous gold wallpaper, 'Bumble Bee' BP525, with carefully matched sawn plywood cupboard fronts.

DECORATING PRINCIPLE 6

Wonderful Wallpaper

Wallpaper by Farrow & Ball introduces texture to a room, as well as colour and the potential for an array of pattern, from the quietly modest 'Polka Square' to the gorgeously flamboyant 'Lotus', from classic stripes and florals to the chic modernity of 'Bamboo'. Made with Farrow & Ball water-based colours, using traditional block-and-trough printing techniques on brush-painted backgrounds, the papers have a handmade, three-dimensional quality that adds tactile allure to their visual appeal.

ABOVE RIGHT This small entrance hall (see pages 64–69) punches far above its weight with the large-scale 'St Antoine' wallpaper in graphic 'Railings' on 'Old White'. Close-hung black and white engravings have enough visual strength to hold their own against this powerful pattern.

BELOW RIGHT AND OPPOSITE BELOW LEFT 'Bumble Bee' BP547 (on the left) and 'Brockhampton Star' BP532 (on the right) add an air of glamour to two cloakrooms. Small in scale, often windowless, but frequently visited, the lavatory is an ideal canvas upon which to experiment with decorating ideas. Lining it with a high-quality wallpaper makes it feel like the interior of a precious casket.

OPPOSITE RIGHT Maud Steengracht (see pages 126–131) has inventively used two different wallpapers in her study – 'Orangerie' BP2501 (seen here) and 'Versailles' BP2614. Surprisingly, the changeover between the two is not immediately noticeable, but the brighter colourway has been used for the walls of the room that receive least natural light, and the effect is to even up the distribution of light and shade in the room.

PAINTING IN THE DETAILS

Giuseppe Cassano is a fortunate man: a successful academic in the field of law, already honoured with the title 'Professore', recently married, good looking, and the owner of a beautiful apartment in central Rome and of a head-turning Maserati. Another of his many achievements is to have succeeded in engaging the services of interior designer Andrea Truglio.

Andrea Truglio is sufficiently in demand not to have to take on new clients. 'I have enough already,' he shrugs. 'Maybe they have a house in town, as well as a house in the country, and a house by the sea. Maybe they buy somewhere new. I am always busy.' However, when Giuseppe called him, he was intrigued. 'Giuseppe told me that his fiancée, Marieangelo, had been collecting cuttings of my work from magazines. He sounded much younger than my usual clients. I agreed to meet him, and as soon as we started talking, there was a rapport, an understanding between us. He has a passion for Italian design, as well as for powerful cars!'

ABOVE LEFT Opposite the front door, a simple shelf, a metal vase, and a pair of black-framed prints establish the mix of the classical and the contemporary that characterizes the decoration of this sleek apartment. The wall is 'Cinder Rose'.

BELOW LEFT The same wall with the front door to the right. The cupboard is painted 'Churlish Green' against walls in 'Dimity'. The rooms to the right of the front door are the reception rooms and kitchen, while to the left are the bedrooms and bathrooms.

RIGHT The dusty pink of 'Cinder Rose' on the wall opposite the front door follows round the corner of the entrance hall, where it contrasts with the 'India Yellow' of the kitchen on the left. The study is straight ahead, the sitting room to the right.

THIS PICTURE The choice of spicy 'India Yellow' for the kitchen is in pointed contrast to the colour palette of the rest of the apartment, which is based on cooler shades of green and purple. In a room of quite stark modernity, with its stainless steel appliances and sharp, contemporary table and chairs, the glow of colour provides a warm welcome.

LEFT Although nicely proportioned, the rooms have lost their original architectural detailing. Andrea has compensated for this lack with a creative use of simple paint effects, such as this horizontal stripe in the living room, which was inspired by the dressed stonework seen on the façades of some Italian palazzos and known as *l'effetto bugnato*. On a colour chart, the shades of off-white look very similar, but used in this way, the lighter 'Dimity' shows up as significantly paler than the background 'Joa's White'. The deep aubergine velvet of the B&B Italia swivel chair and the dusky purple chenille of the sofa find an echo in the 'Cinder Rose' of the walls in the entrance hall glimpsed through the doorway.

ABOVE Elements of pure classicism, such as this plaster copy of a bust of Alexander the Great, seem perfectly at home in the company of sleek, Italian-style modernity.

RIGHT A bronze statuette on a marble plinth stands on a metal console designed by Andrea Truglio.

The next step was for Andrea to visit Giuseppe's apartment. 'The project appealed to me,' Andrea explains, 'not only because I liked Giuseppe and Marieangelo, who are now my very good friends, but because it was starting from nothing. They had virtually no furniture or possessions, aside from Giuseppe's library of academic books, so in terms of design I could create a look for them.'

The space itself was a similarly blank canvas. From the outside, the apartment block is handsome, built in an elegant neoclassical style in the 1930s by Mussolini's favourite architect Marcello Piacentini. These apartments were built for party officials, and they were housed in style. The heavy wooden doors of the ground-floor entrance open to reveal a tiled inner courtyard and a classical fountain. A grand marble staircase encloses

LEFT Oak floorboards add character and flow between rooms, uniting them and making the apartment feel even more spacious. The hot 'India Yellow' of the kitchen can be glimpsed on the left, seen through a doorway in a wall painted 'Cinder Rose', the same colour as the study through the double doors ahead. The remaining two walls of the hallway are 'Dimity'. Guiseppe Cassano's academic books were among the few existing possessions that had to be incorporated into Andrea's design.

the original lift, which rises sedately up and down the building in its ironwork cage. The panelled double doors that open into Giuseppe and Marieangelo's apartment are also original, but behind them the rooms have lost their period features.

Andrea furnished the apartment sparsely but luxuriously, using many of his own designs. But he also gave it back some of the architectural interest and gravitas it had lost, not by importing cornices, architraves, panelling, and picture rails, but by the more simple and economical means of using paint and colour, all chosen from his favoured brand, Farrow & Ball.

After sustained initial consultations, Andrea likes to be left to himself when working on a space for clients. 'I have to understand how they live, and what they like, before I start, but then I become what you might call egoist, fascist even,' he laughs. 'For example, Giuseppe wanted a door that could be closed on the living room, but I insisted it should be a wide

opening, with no door. In this way, you come into the entrance hall and your eye is immediately drawn to the light that comes through this opening, and it feels like an informal welcome. Giuseppe admitted, after I had gone and he had lived in the apartment for a while, that I was completely right.'

The new layout of the apartment is both rational and comfortable. Rooms are arranged in order of privacy, so the hall leads off to the right into the living room with the kitchen opposite it, and the study, where Giuseppe writes, beyond. Unlike the living room, this more secluded space has a door. To your left as you enter the apartment are double doors glazed with frosted glass through which are the two bedrooms and two bathrooms. Oak flooring unites the spaces and some subtle structural changes help the flow of rooms, such as the cutting off at an angle of the corner of a wall in the entrance hall so that the view into the living room is more open.

THIS PAGE AND OPPOSITE ABOVE RIGHT Both the study and the living room open through double, glazed doors onto a covered balcony overlooking a wide street of neoclassical apartment blocks. Here Andrea has added a painted frieze, in lieu of a cornice, in 'Brinjal' on walls of 'Cinder Rose'. Furnishings, including side tables designed by Andrea, are strictly contemporary, aside from a classical bust that looks down from the bookcase and this plaster relief (opposite) above a chair by Flexform.

THIS PAGE The colour scheme of shades of green and purple that predominates throughout the apartment is modified in the main bedroom. Here walls are neutral 'Joa's White', but the bedlinen and cushions continue the theme in mauve and aubergine. The photographs above the bed are by Fiorenzo Niccoli and the bedside lamps are by Louis Poulsen. The bed itself is another Andrea Truglio design, as are the bedside tables.

As for colour, Andrea says he took his cue from the fabric of Marieangelo's favourite handbag, a canvas toile in a dark mauve. Shades of purple, from palest violet 'Cinder Rose' to dusky aubergine 'Brinjal', are contrasted with shades of grey and green throughout the flat, while spicy 'India Yellow' walls distinguish the kitchen. Aside from this culinary hot-spot, the colours are cool, calm, sophisticated, and 'very un-Roman', Andrea says. But what is most interesting about them is the way they are deployed for a quasi-structural effect. In the living room, for example, a previously featureless cube with a window onto the street and a glazed door onto the balcony, Andrea has painted the walls creamy 'Dimity' bisected by thick, horizontal stripes of darker 'Joa's White'. 'It is a simplification of what we call *l'effetto bugnato*,' he explains, 'which describes those horizontal lines of stone on the façade of a palazzo.' Certainly it gives the room a dignity and architectural importance that it would otherwise lack.

In the study – the second most formal of the rooms – a darker stripe of colour makes a border where the walls meet the ceiling and takes on the role of a cornice, and in the second bedroom the wall is divided by five stripes of colours in a contemporary take on the

proportions of classical panelling: the base is a skirting/baseboard in 'Joa's White' with a broad band of 'Cinder Rose' above it to dado level. The remainder of the wall is again 'Dimity' up to a frieze of 'Churlish Green', itself topped by another deep stripe of white at cornice level.

The palette of colours established by the choice of paint is picked up and intensified throughout the apartment in the form of fabrics, curtains, cushions, and the framed photographs that decorate the walls. 'I love colour,' says Andrea, 'because it's so happy.' Newly-weds Giuseppe and Marieangelo would doubtless agree.

LEFT A sleek bathroom in shades of lacquer and 'Joa's White' paint.

ABOVE Andrea has painted the guest bedroom in broad bands of colour, reflecting the classical division of a wall into three areas divided by a dado rail and picture rail. The colours, from the bottom up, are 'Cinder Rose', 'Dimity', and 'Churlish Green'.

DECORATING PRINCIPLE 7

Changing Spaces

Colour and pattern are not simply visually appealing, they are also powerfully transformative elements. Both can be used to disguise awkward proportions as well as highlight architectural beauty. The general rule is that warm colours, based on yellows and reds, seem to advance towards the eye, but cool colours, based on blues and greens, recede. In terms of pattern, a large pattern in a small space creates an illusion of volume, while a small pattern is more enclosing.

ABOVE RIGHT In an apartment that had lost all its original architectural details (see pages 114–121), Andrea Truglio has given the living room visual interest by the simple device of painting thick horizontal bands of 'Joa's White' on a background of 'Dimity'.

BELOW RIGHT Andrea Truglio has introduced the classical proportions more usually provided by skirting/baseboard, dado rail, picture rail, and cornice by using broad stripes of 'Cinder Rose', 'Dimity', and 'Churlish Green'.

BELOW CENTRE The main room of this attic apartment (see pages 80–85) is painted 'All White', except for the end wall, which is 'London Clay'. This dark brown has the effect of foreshortening the space and emphasizes the charm of the roof line, which rises like the inverted hull of a ship.

OPPOSITE The huge ceiling beams in the *salone* of this Italian palazzo (see pages 162–169) are painted 'Book Room Red' to complement the original stencil decoration on the plaster and mirror the brick floor, making a visual link between floor and ceiling that has the effect of bringing the ceiling height down to a more comfortable domestic level.

COUNTRY

From the darkly wooded mountains of Norway to the gentle pastures of Holland, and from the steep vineyards of Umbria to the lush patchwork of the Pays d'Auge, Europe has landscapes of immense variety and beauty, and rural architecture to match. The structures of the following houses could not be more different, as you turn the page from an Italian palazzo with soaring ceilings to a thatched Dutch farmhouse or a Norwegian cabin built from logs. What unites them is a particularly relaxed style of decoration, and the warm, gentle colours of Farrow & Ball.

ABOVE Tongue-and-groove panelled walls in 'Off-White' eggshell and an armoire painted in 'Brinjal' eggshell. **OPPOSITE** Walls in 'New White' with beams painted 'Ball Green'.

THIS PAGE The dining room is in the *bakhuis,* where the baking was originally done, and which has a tiled roof instead of the more flammable thatch that covers the main farmhouse. The walls are lined with tongue-and-groove panelling painted 'Off-White' eggshell, the skirtings/ baseboards and cornice are 'Old White' eggshell, and the window and door frames are 'White Tie' eggshell.

ABOVE A long entrance hall with walls in 'Teresa's Green' Estate Emulsion and doors and door frames in 'White Tie' Full Gloss leads past the kitchen and drawing room to Maud's study. The metal radiator covers, designed and made by Jan, are also 'Teresa's Green' but in Estate Eggshell.

RIGHT The kitchen has floorboards painted in 'Radicchio' Floor Paint. Walls are 'Pavilion Gray', woodwork is 'White Tie', and the kitchen cupboards are 'Matchstick'.

A FAMILY FARM

Maud and Jan Steengracht first met when Jan was studying Law and Maud Law and History of Art. Jan went on to work in land management and Maud for an auction house in The Hague, but both were seeking a way to live a more creative life, and shared a passion for the Dutch countryside. Fifteen years ago, having married and had two daughters, they found a way to combine their talents and enthusiasms by buying a farm and using it as a base from which to run complementary businesses: Jan as a maker of metal furnishings and Maud as a colour consultant and interior decorator.

The farm is on an estate that once belonged to Jan's family. Maud used to come cycling here when she was a little girl. 'My mother would say "we are going to ride our bikes in the most beautiful part of Holland",' she remembers. The landscape surrounding the farm is timeless, criss-crossed with avenues of trees whose roots anchor the banks of the dykes. The wide sky and the flat fields dotted with grazing cows are recognizable from landscape paintings of the 17th century. Maud and Jan's farmhouse seems to have grown naturally out of this peaceful land, sitting long and low under its hood of thatch. Numbers attached to the end gable commemorate the date it was built: 1873. For a small, densely populated country like the Netherlands, this is rural isolation. 'My daughter calls it "the black hole",' laughs Maud, 'because it is so dark at night.'

ABOVE The warm, earthy yellow of 'Hay' gives the drawing room a welcoming glow even on a gloomy day. A pair of 19th-century button-back armchairs, upholstered in rich purple velvet, provide comfortable seating opposite the sofa beneath a portrait of one of Jan's ancestors.

RIGHT The two original doors, one to the hall, the other to the *opkamer* or upper chamber, which is Jan's study, are highlighted in the Archive colour 'Powder Blue'. The more modern double doors on the other side of the room are 'Hay'. The metal table lamp is one of Jan's designs.

When they bought the house in the late 1990s it was a dairy farm lived in by a tenant farmer with five sons, and was messy and unkempt. 'Jan's father asked if the line of the roof was straight,' says Maud. 'Because if it is, the house is structurally sound.' Although the roof was straight, there was a huge amount of restoration to be done. Jan and a builder worked on the house for a year before Maud and the children moved in. 'It was still far from finished,' says Maud. 'I had a sample of silk curtain material and a Farrow & Ball colour card, and I used to carry them around with me and dream

of how lovely it would be when I could decorate.' One of the most traumatic tasks was replacing the thatch. 'We had to move everything out, and when the old thatch was stripped off, the filth was extraordinary. There was a thick layer of black dust, like volcanic ash.'

The group of buildings, which includes a barn, hayloft, stables, and *bakhuis* (bakehouse), still has the feel of a farm, even though the muck and mess are long gone. The house where the farmer lived is at one end of the largest of the buildings, the other end of which was a shippon for the cows.

'The animals were more important than the people when these farms were built,' Maud explains, 'so living accommodation was not a priority.' The front door opens into a long, narrow passage with the kitchen on the left and the drawing room and dining room on the right. At the far end of the passage is a brick-floored room overlooking the rear courtyard. This was once the dairy. 'It is more like a wide corridor or hall,' Maud says, pointing out that no less than six doors lead off it.

This awkward space with its multiple doors is now Maud's study and the fact that it is both cosy and elegant is proof of her skill as a decorator. A high counter, with shelves beneath, separates the body of the room from traffic, and serves as storage for the colour charts, fabric samples, and pattern books that are the tools of Maud's trade. There are bookshelves along one wall incorporating a fitted desk for the computer. The curtains are lined with yellow silk, which Maud chose to reflect warmth into a room that faces north. The masterstroke is the wallpaper, a large-scale, formal design in soft blue and taupe. In fact, it is two different wallpapers, Farrow & Ball's 'Orangerie' on the window wall,

and 'Versailles' on the back wall in a paler version of the same colours. The different but complementary designs add subtle visual variety, while the modulation of colour brings an illusion of brightness to the the darker side of the room.

Maud describes herself as having 'an instinct for colour' inherited from her mother, who is a painter. 'My mother had an artist friend who lived in England, near the Farrow & Ball workshops in Dorset, and she always used their paints on the frames of her pictures. My mother started to do the same, and introduced me to their colours. I have never used anything else since, and always say to my clients that Farrow & Ball is the only paint I will consider for a decorating project.'

Art and craft run through both sides of the family. Jan's mother was a potter, some of whose painted tiles were used in Queen Beatrix's palace. Not long after Jan launched his new business making metal furniture, he had the same honour, when the royal family were photographed sitting on his garden chairs around one of his tables in an image that appeared in all the national papers. Jan and Maud have always collaborated. 'I still have ideas for furnishings that Jan will then put into practice,' says Maud. The house too has been a collaboration. 'My home is my castle,' Maud smiles. 'When we first came here I pinned my hopes on that piece of fabric and paint chart. Now, I am happy.'

ABOVE LEFT Next to the door of the main bedroom, which has walls in 'Setting Plaster' and woodwork in Full Gloss 'White Tie', a wooden door opens into the slope of the main chimney flue, where hams would once have been hung to smoke.

ABOVE RIGHT A wall of this bedroom is lined with cupboards, their doors painted in 'Dove Tale' in eggshell, a colour repeated on the other side of the room on the sloping beams.

OPPOSITE Maud describes her office, which was originally the dairy, as a bit like a corridor, as it has so many doors leading off it, including these double doors in 'Blue Gray'; the one on the left opening onto a short flight of steps up to Jan's study, the other onto stairs down to the cellar. Maud has used two different designs of wallpaper in the room, 'Versailles' BP2614 on this wall and the back wall, which is the darkest part of this north-facing room, and the lighter, brighter 'Orangerie' BP2501 on remaining walls.

RIGHT A cloakroom in 'Teresa's Green' above wall tiles made by Jan's mother.

LEFT The house is part of the largest and most imposing structure in this picturesque Normandy village; a building that was originally a monastery and then a school of astronomy before being divided to make a row of terraced homes on four storeys. The exterior paintwork is 'Dimity'.

RIGHT Juliette has opened up the ground floor to make a large living and dining room. Creamy 'Dimity' on the ceiling and woodwork and soft grey 'Elephant's Breath' on the walls complement the pale stone of the 17th-century chimneybreast.

OVERLEAF Painted in sophisticated 'Charleston Gray', the entrance hall opens into the ground-floor living room, with its dining area and comfortable seating to the left of the table around the fireplace. A reclaimed door ahead hides the fuse box/distribution board.

A ROYAL WELCOME

Juliette Bartillat is an interior decorator based in Paris. But despite her high heels and leather jacket, and her enviable aura of Parisian chic, she is equally at home in the country, where she has a house with a large garden, grows vegetables, and keeps chickens. The area of Normandy where Juliette retreats from city life is as pretty as the illustrations in a book of nursery rhymes, with villages of half-timbered, steeply gabled cottages and spiked church steeples set among the gentle swell of hills, woods, and hedges.

The village of Beaumont-en-Auge is particularly charming, its main street a patchwork of ancient houses painted in shades of blue, green, brown, and rust between the vertical stripes of their wooden frames. Walls are draped in Virginia creeper, windows framed by geraniums and shutters; there are tiny dormers in mansard roofs, mini gardens on metal balconies, and even the pavements are picturesque herringbone brick.

OPPOSITE At the front of the house on the first floor is a long living room that was used as a dormitory when the house was a school of astronomy. Here, as in all the upstairs rooms, Juliette has painted the walls, beams, and timber framing in warm off-white 'Dimity'. Furnishings are an imaginative mix of the antique, the reproduction, and the contemporary.

In the middle of the village, next to the church, is a tall, pale stone building, notable for its relative grandeur. Along its wisteria-fringed frontage, narrow flower-beds sprout towering hollyhocks, feathery fennel, and lavender, and in the midst of the foliage a door opens into Juliette Bartillat's third home.

Step inside and you are greeted by an array of interesting and decorative objects, arranged with the eye of a professional decorator. On the wall opposite the door hang four antique and vintage mirrors, one oblong, one oval, one round, one trapezoid, and below them is a side table on which are displayed four turquoise raku glaze pots, two propped-up seascapes, a wooden trough, a walking stick topped by a carved bird, a striped ceramic dish holding three oriental metal counters, a metal ruler, and a guest book. There is also a large piece of slate with a handwritten message: 'Welcome to the Maison du Collège Royal. Would you be kind enough not to remove and be careful with all the decoration items that I left in the house to make your stay as pleasant as possible...Feel free to leave me a message on this book...Enjoy your stay. Kindly, Juliette.'

The country house where Juliette lives is a short moped ride away. This is an extra; a house she could not resist buying and restoring, and which she now rents out as an unusually stylish and comfortable holiday home. As requested, guests have written in her book comments such as 'it is quite unique the way you manage to combine the sensation of history with modern comforts' and complimenting her on the homemade bread, the cider and apple juice, and the 'amazing bed linen and towels'.

Only a few years ago, reviews of the house might have been rather different. 'It had been for sale for a long time when I bought it,' Juliette reveals.

ABOVE The open-plan kitchen area is given its own distinctive decorative character with the use of warm red 'Blazer' for the walls, against which these shelves painted in 'Railings' make a graphic contrast.

LEFT The 17th-century wooden staircase, with its comically low banister rail, winds its way up the centre of the house, and is one of its most charming features. Juliette has boxed off the area below the stairs and added a reclaimed door to make a utility room and cloakroom.

'It was lived in by the same couple for 30 years and had been decorated in horrible, garish colours. The kitchen was in a small room at the back on the first floor and, although the old staircase and the panelling were intact, the interior looked very ugly indeed.' But beyond and beneath the ugliness, Juliette could see the intrinsic beauty of the architecture.

Originally a monastery, the building was severely damaged by fire in the 18th century, after which, by order of the king, it was converted into a college of astronomy. When the school closed it was divided to make a row of terraced, four-storey houses. Stripped back by Juliette to reveal the ancient timbers of internal walls and ceilings and the polished clay floor tiles,

the history of these rooms, and the changes they have undergone over the centuries, is now apparent. There is a 17th-century stone fireplace in the ground-floor living room, and a second living room spans the house at the front of the first floor, and is lit by six slim windows with panelling beneath. On the floor above, the main bedroom features a fine carved wooden chimneypiece and overmantel. Ceilings are high, and even though the walls are thick, they are pierced by so many windows that every room is bathed in light. Linking the floors and running up the middle of the house is a winding wooden staircase, its quaintly low banister and narrow treads worn to a sheen by generations of hands and feet.

All traces of the garish colours have disappeared under shades of Farrow & Ball; 'Elephant's Breath' in the downstairs living room, 'Blazer' in the kitchen, 'Charleston Gray' in the hall, and creamy 'Dimity' on the beams and walls of the bedrooms. Furnishings are both simple and sophisticated, as befits a building of this architectural status in a rustic setting. Using clever combinations of the old and the new, the real and the ersatz, the antique and the fake, Juliette has created interiors of style and interest, more like a home than a rental property.

Although there are plenty of lovely places to visit nearby, including glorious chateaux and the beaches at Deauville and Trouville, examining the pictures and the various decorative items that are arranged on furniture, mantelpieces, and windowsills throughout the house could happily fill a rainy holiday afternoon. In the first-floor living room, for example, the pictures include a 19th-century oil portrait in a modern frame, an old engraving of Venice in an antique frame, and a modern print on metal of a painting by Corot that looks at first glance like an expensive original. A bowl on the reproduction Regency table holds five terracotta money boxes sculpted as heads, and there is a pair of antique wooden legs on the shelves behind. Just as the note on the hall table promises, these are the finishing touches that – along with the location, the architecture, and the comfort – make this house such a pleasure to stay in.

ABOVE Another view of the first-floor living room shows the six windows that march across the façade of this impressive building. They allow in so much light that the fact that in summer three of them are shaded by a green veil of wisteria doesn't matter. The pictures that hang between the windows include original oils, antique prints, and modern reproductions. The notched beam in the old terracotta tiled floor shows where there would once have been a wooden partition.

TOP The flat-screen television at one end of the living room is a visual counterpoint to the ancient timbers of its setting, just as the warm pulses of the deep red cushions and paisley throw have added impact in a decorative scheme that is uniformly white 'Dimity'.

ABOVE A view from the second-floor landing into the main bedroom. The steep, narrow staircase continues up another flight to two attic bedrooms.

OPPOSITE The main bedroom is on the second floor and stretches from the front to the back of the house with three windows onto the street and two onto the garden. Walls and beams are 'Dimity', although the polished walnut of the carved 18th-century fireplace and overmantel have been left unpainted. The grey carpet, soft grey and mauve linen bedclothes, and dark green of the velvet cushions combine for a particularly calming colour scheme.

ABOVE LEFT The gentle interplay between the colours of natural wood, stone, and terracotta and the colour and texture of painted surfaces is apparent in this view from the main bedroom to the landing and stairs.

ABOVE RIGHT The second bedroom on this floor is dominated by a huge armoire that Juliette has painted in 'Railings', a glimpse of which can just be seen reflected in one of the mirrors that hangs above the bedside table. Walls and their timber framing are painted in 'Dimity'.

BELOW RIGHT On the same floor is the main bathroom, made in a room that was once another bedroom. Here, as elsewhere, the uniform paint colour 'Dimity' serves to sew together the disparate architectural elements of an interior that has been chopped and changed over the centuries.

DECORATING PRINCIPLE 8

Alfresco Painting

First impressions tend to stick, which is why estate agents/realtors often advise a fresh coat of paint for your front door to seduce prospective buyers before they even step over the threshold. The choice of colour for exterior doors, window frames, balconies, railings, and shutters can transform the appearance of a house, and enhance or detract from its architecture. The stronger the colour contrast, the more attention will be drawn to particular features.

ABOVE RIGHT A farmhouse granary in the Norwegian mountains (see pages 144–151) has been converted to make a guest bedroom. Its front door is 'Lamp Room Gray', while the decorative woodwork is highlighted in 'Pointing'.

RIGHT The 'Green Smoke' of the shutters and glazing bars of this Georgian house in Spitalfields (see pages 26–33) may not be strictly authentic but has the right period feel.

CENTRE Juliette Bartillat's garden shed looks chic and also discreet under a coat of 'Railings' with garden furniture painted to match (see also pages 132–141).

OPPOSITE ABOVE RIGHT Using the same paint colour inside as out creates a seamless continuity. Here, warm 'Dimity' blends with the pale, honey stonework of Juliette Bartillat's village house in Normandy.

OPPOSITE BELOW RIGHT Hand-forged metal handles stand out against 'Shaded White' on the door to Eva Gnaedinger's house (see pages 96–103). Built in the 1970s, the building is not architecturally distinguished, but this subtle grey against walls of shadowy brown 'Mouse's Back' gives it an air of modest sophistication.

LIVING THE HIGH LIFE

For weeks at a time in the summer, for Christmas, and whenever they tire of city living, Liv and Jan Krogstad climb into their four-wheel drive and set off north on the wide, empty roads beyond Oslo towards the mountains. The drive itself is a pleasure; curving through woods of regal Norwegian pines with trunks as straight and tall as ships' masts, along the edge of glassy lakes and broad rivers, passing through tunnels in the rock, always slowly climbing, until they reach the small village, 750 metres/2500 feet above sea level, where they have their country home.

OPPOSITE ABOVE The farm occupies an idyllic position above a small village. The cluster of wooden buildings, with traditional turf roofs, comprises a guest house and workshop on the right, with the farmhouse and granary on slightly higher ground to the left.

OPPOSITE BELOW LEFT In between regular trims, the roofs grow shaggy with long grasses and wild flowers, here sheltering a pair of diminutive windows.

OPPOSITE BELOW CENTRE The old granary or *stolpehus*, now a guest bedroom, is raised on stones to protect its contents from vermin.

OPPOSITE BELOW RIGHT A display of traditional Norwegian painted plates, carved breadboards, and spoons hangs against the wooden walls of the kitchen painted in 'Lichen'.

RIGHT The entrance hall, staircase, and bedroom above are a new extension and lead to the kitchen, which occupies part of the original farmhouse. The boarded walls and ceiling are 'Pointing'. The stair rail is 'Mahogany' with stair treads in 'Lamp Room Gray' and risers in 'Dead Salmon'.

RIGHT The old farmhouse was originally two separate rooms downstairs, but a wide opening has been cut in the wooden wall to link the kitchen with the living room, both of which are painted 'Lichen'. A ladder staircase on the left leads up to an open mezzanine under the pitch of the roof, now used as a bedroom for visiting grandchildren.

ABOVE The double height of the guest-house kitchen, a building reconstructed from the timbers of a demolished barn, is halved at one end by a wooden ceiling with a landing and bedroom above and a second bedroom below. This main room is painted 'French Gray' with doors and ceiling beams in 'Pointing'. The glow of the 'India Yellow' bedroom can be seen through the open door.

LEFT At the other end of the guest kitchen, a window above the painted dresser affords a view of the grassy slopes of the workshop roof. The brass wall sconces are also Norwegian and antique.

ABOVE The faint smell of woodsmoke from the corner fireplace scents the living room and kitchen. The colour scheme of 'Lichen' and 'Pointing' has a traditional feel in a house that would always have had painted walls, and combines with the brown leather and English woollen upholstery to reflect the colours of nature beyond the windows; even the touches of red are echoed by the glistening ruby of the late-summer redcurrants that festoon the bushes outside the kitchen door.

Liv and Jan already knew the area, as Liv's parents also had a second home here. When they bought the house in the early 1990s they were still living in England. 'We were looking for somewhere we could go for holidays in Norway and we borrowed three Norwegian newspapers from friends and found it for sale in a tiny little advertisement,' Liv remembers. 'Jan flew over to see it and took some videos. We all loved the look of it and immediately agreed we should buy it. It wasn't very much money and it was in a wonderful location.'

In truth, it would be difficult to imagine any location more wonderful. Surrounded on three sides by meadows, its back tucked against a rocky slope, the house stands above the village with views far into the distance down a valley of steeply scooped hills, their edges serrated by the dark silhouettes of trees. Sun glances off the polished surface of water along the base of the valley, while in the other direction snow wraps the peaks of distant mountains even in the height of summer. Sheep graze on grass thick with harebells, violets, scabious, and clover. The gentle clank of their bells and the rush of water from the stream that passes the gate are the only sounds. In winter there is silence.

Built as a farm at the turn of the last century, the house is as picturesque as its location is majestic. There are three buildings, closely grouped inside a traditional fence of

diagonal birch staves. Walls are weathered wooden logs, and the pitched roofs are carpeted with grass and wild flowers, as if pieces of the surrounding meadow had levitated like verdant magic carpets and landed on them. Next to the main house is a small *stolpehus* – a wooden hut balanced on squat stone legs, once used to store foodstuffs and grain safe from vermin. In front, slightly lower down the hill, is a guest house. Birch bark lines the edges of the turf roofs, and chains hang from the corners to direct rain and melting ice into wooden barrels. The gate posts are two stone menhirs, and there are redcurrant bushes glistening with bright bunches of fruit in the garden.

'Everyone thought we were mad when we bought it,' Liv admits. 'It was in very bad condition and the main house only had two rooms downstairs with an attic in the pitch of the roof.' A black and white photograph dating back to 1910 when the house was first built shows

LEFT AND ABOVE Stairs lead down from the hall of the guest annexe to a room beneath its kitchen built into the slope of the land. This is a room for winter evenings, its sense of cosy enclosure enhanced by the warm 'Ointment Pink' on panelling, woodwork, and walls.

OPPOSITE Suspended under the apex of the roof, over the middle of the living room, this wooden platform is a room for visiting grandchildren, its walls in 'Lichen' and its ceiling supported by the roughly carved trunks of pines painted in 'Pointing', as are the floorboards.

LEFT On the first floor of the new extension to the farmhouse is a bedroom with traditional wooden box beds fitted under the sloping eaves. The woodwork of the beds and the wood-lined walls are painted 'Parma Gray', a soft, elusive shade that looks more blue than grey the stronger the light. The gingham bedcovers and red floral blinds contribute to the country, folk art feel.

OPPOSITE ABOVE LEFT The downstairs bedroom in the guest annexe is almost filled by a modern four-poster made to a traditional Norwegian design, with two duvets laid side by side instead of one, for extra warmth. The planked walls are 'India Yellow', a spicy mustard hue often seen used on the exterior of barns and houses in the Norwegian countryside as an alternative to the equally common oxblood red.

OPPOSITE ABOVE RIGHT In the same bedroom, an antique Norwegian desk retains its original paint finish in deep maroon and peacock green. The fresh white of the window frame in 'Pointing' is matched by crisp, checked voile curtains.

the farmer, his wife, and son in traditional Norwegian costume, proudly posed in front of it surrounded by shaggy hayricks. More recently, two generations of the same farming family shared the house, one family in the room that is now the kitchen, one in the living room. They left some pieces of furniture when they moved, including the painted grandfather clock that still stands in the living room and a painted dresser now in the guest house.

Jan and Liv have slowly and respectfully restored and extended over the years. They replaced the original barn using timber from another old building in the village, which was taken apart and reassembled to make what is now the guest house. The *stolpehus* has also been converted to make

a bedroom with its own diminutive bathroom, and the main house has been enlarged with the addition of a new wing containing an entrance hall, a utility room, and cloakroom, and a bedroom under the eaves.

Norway has strong regional folk art traditions, which the architecture of the house reflects. And while Liv and Jan's apartment in Oslo (see pages 34–41) displays a collection of striking contemporary artworks, here the furnishings include many pieces of antique Norwegian painted furniture. Also traditional is the fact that the wooden walls of the interior are almost all painted and, although the colours are not strictly based on historical precedent, they reflect and complement the colours that reoccur on the painted furniture.

'India Yellow', for example, which they have used both in the guest house and in the main house, is the same shade of ochre that lines the dresser shelves in the guest-house kitchen. A similar colour is often used to paint the exterior of old wooden buildings, and is as familiar a sight in the Norwegian countryside as the equally traditional oxblood red.

In the bigger spaces of the main house and guest house, Liv has chosen soft, smoky 'French Gray', 'Pointing', and 'Parma Gray'. 'They are such versatile paints,' she says. 'In Oslo they are the perfect background for modern paintings and photographs, and here they seem to have just the right organic feel for an old building made of wood.'

RIGHT At the other end of the guest annexe from the 'India Yellow' bedroom is a bathroom painted in the same colour. When first available in England in the 18th-century, this pigment was made by reducing the urine of cows fed on mango leaves. It is similar to yellow ochre, a natural earth pigment more likely to have been the source of the colour traditionally used on Norwegian farm buildings.

GRAND ILLUSIONS

Maisons-Laffitte, a town on the Seine about 11 miles north west of the centre of Paris, is known in France as 'la cité du cheval'. A hundred years ago, the racecourse here and the one in Newmarket in England were the two finest in the world. Although its global significance has dwindled, the Maisons-Laffitte racecourse still thrives and gives the town its identity. Horse racing is what Maisons-Laffitte is famous for. That, and the quintessentially French image of its 17th-century chateau, the exquisite façade of which greets visitors as they cross the river into the town from Paris.

ABOVE Adjoining the house, accessed through a gate at the side, ranks of stables surround a sandy courtyard from where Philippe Alric's shouted instructions to expert riders can be heard: '*allez, allez....redemande simplement....très bien!*'

LEFT No one would guess that this drawing room, with its antique stone chimneypiece, is in fact a new extension. Antique double doors open onto the hall of the original building, where a wall of reclaimed *boiseries* incorporates a door to the cloakroom. Several different shades of off-white – 'Shaded White' for the walls, 'Great White' for the ceiling, and 'All White' for the beams – contribute to the faded elegance.

RIGHT The kitchen is a masterly work of disguise. Set into walls painted in practical 'Archive' Modern Emulsion, as opposed to the Estate Emulsion used elsewhere, are reclaimed panelled doors that conceal the fridge and other storage.

ABOVE Against the kitchen wall opposite the fridge are an antique sideboard, table, and wall cupboard, all painted 'Blue Gray'. The only obviously 21st-century intrusions in this room are the range cooker and a coffee maker. Everything else is hidden in baskets and under antique linen napkins.

ABOVE LEFT French doors open from the dining room onto a terrace and lawn, beyond which is the exercise yard of Philippe's riding school. Before the drawing room extension was built, this was the living room. Here the walls and ceiling are 'Pointing', while the furnishings epitomize French 'shabby chic' and include an 18th-century glazed cabinet with what remains of its original paint.

OPPOSITE The 'Shaded White' of the drawing room, which is the lighter of the two rooms thanks to its row of arched, glazed doors from an 18th-century orangery, is a couple of tones darker than the 'Pointing' of the dining room.

At the turn of the 20th century, an American millionaire and racehorse owner, Frank Jay Gould, built stables and a riding school here, conveniently close to the racecourse. The spacious yard where his horses were trained and exercised was separated from the road by high railings and entered through elaborate iron gates flanked by a pair of half-timbered Anglo-Norman pavilions. Rows of stables ran along two sides of the yard, and there was a house at one end where the stable lads lived. In the park on the other side of the road, Mr Gould erected a bronze statue of his champion racehorse Dollar.

During the Second World War, the area was badly bombed and the stables were destroyed. The site was abandoned, the remaining buildings gradually fell into disrepair, and squatters moved in. Then, some 20 years ago, a young couple fell in love with the place, saw beyond the dereliction, and decided they would like to buy it. International Eventing rider and instructor Philippe Alric and antiques dealer Sophie Lambert planned to restore the whole site, making it a home for their family but also a business for Philippe, who would run it as a riding school and livery stables.

Fortunately, Philippe and Sophie were fiercely determined. It took them ten years to get the right permissions to enable them to buy the buildings. Another 13 years on and it is evident that their persistence, hard work, and style have paid off handsomely. The stables are now fully occupied, the two half-timbered pavilions are a clubhouse and an

OPPOSITE The coffee table in the drawing room is made from an old planked door resting on low trestles, which Sophie has painted in 'Pigeon' and distressed with a dilute solution of *bitume de judée.*

ABOVE LEFT The main bedroom is above the drawing room, its network of beams supporting a mansard roof punctuated by dormer windows. As elsewhere upstairs, the floorboards are painted, in this room in 'Skimming Stone', an off-white with no undertones of green or yellow and slightly darker than the 'Wimborne White' that has been used for the walls.

ABOVE RIGHT Slotted under the eaves, round the corner from the chimney flue against which the bed is placed, are a bathtub and sink, the underside of the tub in 'Skimming Stone' to match the floor and beams.

antiques showroom, and the house has been extended, refitted, and furnished in the elegant, pale Gustavian style that is Sophie's trademark.

Sophie's shop, *Au Temps des Cerises*, is a few miles away in Saint-Germain-en-Laye, and sells a seductive mix of 18th-century distressed painted furniture, much of it Swedish, gilt clocks and mirrors, pastel portraits, and an acreage of antique French linens. The colour palette of the shop is every shade of white except brilliant, and the effect is of expensively bleached and faded elegance.

If Sophie's shop sells the ingredients for a particular look, her house is the finished confection, and the ultimate advertisement for her style and how to translate it into a series of picture-perfect interiors. Designed as accommodation for the stable lads, the building was originally modest in size and very plain, with a narrow wooden staircase leading to small bedrooms. Character and beauty have been entirely imported, not only in the shape of antique tables, chairs, sofas, chests, and armoires, but also more structural elements such as fireplaces, doors, windows, and panelling.

Sophie and Philippe's most recent addition to the house is an extension that has created a large drawing room and, above it, a main bedroom and bathroom. Central to the design of the drawing room are three arched and glazed doors from an 18th-century orangery. Even older is the carved stone chimneypiece, also reclaimed, which faces them from the opposite wall. Through glazed double doors to the right of the chimneybreast, you can see into the entrance hall, its far wall lined with 18th-century panelling of honey-coloured wood, stained almost white in places by the ingrained inlay of its

original paint. Seamlessly incorporated, these borrowed architectural features give the house the atmosphere of a much older, much grander building.

Through a wide opening on the other side of the drawing room fireplace is the dining room. Here again there is an antique stone fireplace, complemented by antique doors connecting with the kitchen beyond. As for the kitchen itself, the only signs that the 21st century has dawned are the shiny range cooker by La Cornue and the discreetly placed electric kettle and coffee maker. The fridge is disguised behind an old, carved door, its once-glazed upper panels veiled with chicken wire backed by antique linen, and the fitted storage cupboards are fronted by folding doors that once connected rooms in a chateau. Pans are hidden on shelves behind indigo-dyed antique linen curtains, rubber gloves are tucked away in a wicker basket under the sink, crockery is stored in an antique wall cupboard, and even the dish-rack is padded with an indigo-dyed, antique monogrammed linen napkin.

Sophie's taste for subtle, muted colour is perfectly served by the Farrow & Ball palette of neutral hues, and she has used a selection of them throughout the house, not only on walls and woodwork, but also on some pieces of furniture. In the kitchen, the walls are 'String' and the antique sideboard and wall cupboard above are 'Blue Gray'. In the drawing room, the walls are 'Shaded White', the ceiling beams are 'All White', and the 18th-century bookcase is 'Great White', while the top of the coffee table made from old planks on trestles is 'Pigeon'. Upstairs, walls are 'New White', beams 'Off White', and the floorboards are 'Old White'. Only the children's bedrooms diverge from the pale stone palette, with 'Calamine' on Violette's walls and masculine 'Eating Room Red' on the beams and floorboards of teenage César's attic hide-out.

'I absolutely love Farrow & Ball paints,' Sophie confirms. 'The tones are very subtle and change according to the light, and the matt, powdery finish pleases me hugely. I would never use anything else!'

ABOVE 'Calamine', used on the walls of Violette's bedroom, is one of the palest pinks in the Farrow & Ball range and, just like the old-fashioned lotion it is named after, can look almost white in some lights. The floor is 'Old White' and the antique cupboard is 'London Stone', both extremely subtle neutrals.

LEFT 'Old White' has also been used for the floor of the landing, where the walls are 'New White' and the ceiling beams 'Old White'. Stairs painted in 'Eating Room Red' lead up to teenage César's attic bedroom.

THIS PAGE Perhaps appropriately in a house with such a distinctly feminine feel, César's top-floor bedroom is the only room that deviates from a palette of soft, pale shades of white and neutral. Here full-blooded 'Eating Room Red' marks out the grid of beams against walls of 'Elephant's Breath', and has also been used on the floorboards and the underside of the bathtub that stands on tiled flooring at one end of the room.

DECORATING PRINCIPLE 9

Light Relief

White paint never goes completely out of fashion because its effect is as reliably and perennially chic as a little black dress. While bright white can be both unforgiving and bland, a mix of off-whites (see pages 180–185) is a fail-safe recipe for calm sophistication. Farrow & Ball offers 30 to 40 shades, depending on how 'white' you like your whites to be.

ABOVE RIGHT In Juliette Bartillat's house in Normandy, the rich strawberry of the rug, the quilted throw, and two cushions (not seen) provide vivid 'pops' of bold colour in a room that is painted 'Dimity' (see pages 132–141). This off-white with the tiniest hint of a red base colour also flatters the clay tile flooring.

OPPOSITE Red again appears as highlights in the airy, relaxing space of Sophie Lambert's attic bedroom (see pages 152–159). Here walls are 'Wimborne White' and the beams and floor are 'Skimming Stone', both off-whites with a contemporary feel and a lilac base, which is why the purples in the rug look so good with them. Matched with antique linens, the effect is refined and timeless.

BELOW CENTRE Black and white is a classic combination that looks at its best when the white is not too bright and the black is not too harsh. In a bathroom painted in 'Dimity', Juliette Bartillat has created a simple arrangement of items on a dark metal table. This, along with the monochrome pictures in dark wood frames above, forms a smart and satisfying composition of silhouettes.

RIGHT Painting furniture the same colour as the walls and woodwork creates a seamless effect. In this bedroom in my own house (see pages 170–177), creamy 'White Tie' on the walls and the chest of drawers provides a serene background for books and ornaments.

COLLECTED
WORKS

'My house is in the centre of Foligno, which is in the centre of Umbria, which is in the centre of Italy, which – of course – is the centre of the world!' Antonello Radi has a sense of humour that is as infectious as his laugh. Although he is not entirely serious when he claims that all roads lead to Foligno, he has a deep love for the part of Italy in which he was born, and an intense appreciation of its beauty.

OPPOSITE Double doors framed by curtains open from the first-floor arcaded terrace into the main *salone* of this 16th-century palazzo. The rough lime plaster of the walls is painted in 'Joa's White', while the huge ceiling beams are 'Book Room Red'. A leather sofa and velvet-covered armchairs are grouped around the vast stone fireplace, which Antonello has filled with dozens of candles.

ABOVE Furnishings, such as this 17th-century chest in the *salone*, are almost exclusively Italian, mostly from Umbria or Tuscany. The 14th-century painting of the Madonna and Child, with applied metal crowns, would once have been displayed in a church, and has been blackened by centuries of candle smoke.

FAR LEFT The terrace outside the entrance to the apartment is sheltered by an arcaded roof. The walls are 'Setting Plaster'.

LEFT The stencilled decoration on the ceiling of the *salone* is original, but the beams have been repainted, their warm 'Book Room Red' a counterbalance to the strawberry glow of the polished brick flooring.

Foligno is a town in a wide river plain with the peaks of the Apennines rising behind it, and a circlet of medieval towns and villages around it. Due to its importance as a hub for Italy's railway system, the town was extensively bombed in World War II. Despite the destruction, it has been left with a number of important medieval and Renaissance buildings that Antonello is keen to point out, including the Palazzo Orfini, where the first printed edition of Dante's *Divine Comedy* was produced in the 15th century, the gorgeously frescoed offices of Antonello's family's banking business, and Antonello's own splendid apartment in the principal rooms of a 16th-century palazzo.

From the outside, the only clue to the architectural grandeur of this last interior is the ornately carved Renaissance stonework that frames the windows of the *piano nobile*. Heavy, studded double doors open

LEFT AND ABOVE The kitchen leads directly off the *salone* and is painted 'Lime White'. The door between the two rooms retains its original pink and green paint, discovered beneath later layers. Antonello loves the patina of antique paint and the way that Farrow & Ball paints, with their handmade feel, complement it. This room has always been the kitchen, but the built-in cupboards and antique Sicilian wall tiles are Antonello's additions.

THIS PAGE At the other end of the kitchen, more of Antonello's collection of *cocci* are displayed on a 16th-century cupboard. The folding table is also 16th century.

from the street into a wide tunnel that leads to a brick-paved inner courtyard. From here, marble stairs climb to Antonello's private entrance. When this second pair of thick double doors opens, it takes the eyes a moment to adjust from the dazzle of the Italian sun to the shadowy interior of a room that is baronial in scale, with a soaring ceiling and a massive stone chimneypiece that rises between tall windows at the far end.

'It is small,' says Antonello, and this time he is not joking. 'There is only this *salone*, and two rooms either side. I am thinking of buying the apartment next door so I can have more space.' Size is relative, and Antonello has a larger house nearby with a garden where he spends much of his time – 'I am a slave to gardening,' he says. In truth, it isn't that he needs more space, but that he would hugely enjoy filling it. 'I am a maximalist,' he announces, proudly, gesticulating around this enormous room. 'After I restored the building, I furnished it in just one year.' A tour of the apartment – a kitchen and small *salone* flanking one side of the main room, a bedroom and a bathroom the other – confirms that Antonello must be the antiques-buying equivalent of a Formula 1 racing driver.

The furniture, paintings, and decorative objects are predominantly Italian, mostly Umbrian. The exceptions are some of the rugs and cushions, which are Moroccan, and the shells and corals, drawn from all over the world. A long refectory table stretching across the *salone* greets visitors with a taste of things to come. Arranged on it, as if ready to be painted by a 17th-century Dutch master, are two huge white corals, a vast terracotta pot holding branches hung with rosehips, a pair of engraved platters the size of car wheels, a towering gilt metal candlestick, and an antique red coral on a stand. Beyond, a smaller table holds more coral, more candlesticks, and pieces of maiolica pottery. The kitchen houses an extraordinary collection of 17th- and 18th-century kitchenware, including cooking pots with their original wire mesh casings, colanders, and jars for oil, water, and wine. The bathroom is

OPPOSITE AND RIGHT Next to the kitchen is the small *salone*, where the walls are 'Porphyry Pink' to match the terracotta tones in the ceiling frescoes (right), which depict figures representing the continents of Europe, Asia, Africa, and America. Furnishings include a 16th-century cupboard from a monastery with its original pale blue paint and a pair of 19th-century chairs with their original chenille upholstery.

ABOVE The terracotta pink of the walls makes an effective background to a patchwork of pictures, which includes work by living artists as well as prints and oil paintings dating from the 17th to the 19th centuries.

TOP AND ABOVE Antonello built a huge bathtub inspired by ancient Roman baths. The walls are 'Dimity' Estate Emulsion with a border at floor level of 'Tunsgate Green'. The mirror frames above the antique stone basins are 'Porphyry Pink' and the birdcage is 18th-century Florentine in front of a window in 'Dorset Cream'.

bristling with yet more coral and shells, the bedroom houses a rare carved 17th-century cassone, a medieval crucifix, an 18th-century processional lantern, and two 16th-century Siennese prie-dieux as bedside tables. There are birdcages in every room and every surface holds an arrangement of objects dating from the 16th to the 19th centuries.

Antonello's passion for collecting has turned him into a self-taught connoisseur. 'I do not fall in love with a piece because of its rarity or value,' he says, 'but because of the energy it transmits – energy from all those years of use. I love to use my antiques.' True to his word, he serves tea in 18th-century pottery cups. He is also a passionate advocate of patina. 'It is the manifestation of history. So I will clean a piece, but nothing more.' This tolerance of the worn, chipped, flaking, even the broken extends to his restoration of these grand old rooms, two of which have frescoed ceilings. He has left the kitchen beams unpainted in order 'to respect the smoke of 500 years', as he puts it. He has scraped later paint off door surrounds to reveal 18th-century marbling, and he chose Farrow & Ball paints because he likes their handmade feel. 'The colours have an organic, simple beauty that looks right next to the old paint.' The 'Porphyry Pink' in the small *salone* and the 'Blue Ground' in the bedroom were both chosen to complement the colours of the late 18th-century painted ceilings, while the 'Book Room Red' of the massive ceiling beams in the *salone* matches the red of the original stencilled decoration on the plaster between them.

Having trained as a lawyer, Antonello now devotes his time to artistic pursuits, including figurative paintings and interior decoration for friends and clients. He recently launched 'Il Bucovita', a lifestyle store in New York where you can buy Italian antiques, and the work of traditional Italian craftsmen including stone and marble basins, terracotta tiles, glassware, carving, and handmade candles. 'Simple things, but beautiful,' says Antonello.

THIS PAGE AND OPPOSITE ABOVE RIGHT The 'Blue Ground' of the bedroom was again chosen to match colours in the decoration of the domed ceiling. Like the bathroom, this room has a painted skirting/baseboard, here in 'Vert de Terre' separated from the blue by a thin line of 'Charleston Gray'. The carved cassone at the foot of the bed is 17th century, and the prie-dieux on either side of the bed are 16th-century Siennese.

OUR HOUSE

As I was writing the section of this book entitled 'Dark Drama', it occurred to me that it was about time I took my own advice. We have a 'small and badly-lit' inner hall and it was painted white. Surely we were missing an opportunity by not painting it something deliciously dusky instead? As soon as I thought of it, I couldn't wait. We got our hands on some 'Mahogany' Estate Eggshell the same weekend and set to work. And, just as I had promised, the result was exciting and theatrical. Anything placed against it took on new vibrancy, whether the self-portrait our daughter painted for an art examination or the plaster relief that had been languishing unappreciated on a windowsill. The hall has a faint air of mystery, and it still gives me a thrill every time I walk through it.

OPPOSITE ABOVE The end wall of the kitchen is filled by a fitted dresser, built around an old sideboard by local joiner Peter Bennett. 'Mouse's Back' makes a pleasing neutral background for the motley collection of old blue-and-white china in the middle and plates in other colours in the glazed cupboards on either side. The door to the inner hall standing open on the right is 'Mahogany'.

ABOVE We inherited a colour scheme of blue and cream in this room, which we have repainted using 'String' and 'Cook's Blue'. The Aga dates back to the 1940s.

ABOVE RIGHT The use of gloss paint in a kitchen is typical of old farmhouses in the West Country, chosen for its durability and because it can be wiped. This kitchen window looks out over a cobbled courtyard where there is a Tudor well.

RIGHT Lining paper covered the wall at this end of the kitchen and the mottled remains of old layers of paint underneath were so pretty that we have left them. The matchboard panelling is painted in 'String'.

LEFT This small inner hall is lit by a tiny window cut into an ancient back door and borrowed light from the kitchen, entrance hall, downstairs cloakroom, and drawing room that all lead off it. Recently, we decided to paint it dark 'Mahogany', which has made the experience of passing through it far more exciting and its contents look far more interesting.

ABOVE Looking back from the drawing room through the same inner hall, you can see how closely the 'Mahogany' paintwork matches the 17th-century dark oak panelling of this room. You can also see the vibrant 'Saxon Green' of the entrance hall.

It would be rather odd to have written two books about Farrow & Ball paints and wallpapers without being something of an aficionado. I have been one for more than 20 years, ever since we painted our first house in Greenwich, London with 'String', 'Light Blue', and 'Old White'. Our next house was 'Old White' and 'String', and in this house we have really pushed the boat out, with a hall in the Archive colour 'Saxon Green', a library in 'London Stone', a bedroom in 'Light Blue', a bedroom in 'String', a study in 'Blue Gray', a kitchen in 'Cook's Blue', 'String', and 'Mouse's Back', and now an inner hall in 'Mahogany'. Everything else is 'White Tie'.

What is often referred to as the 'knocked-back' quality of Farrow & Ball colours suits this house, which is old, well-worn, and sturdily rooted in the middle of a small Devon town. Even freshly applied, a Farrow & Ball colour has an innate modesty that makes it look settled and as though it might have been there for some time. We have also changed colours, not just 'White Tie' to 'Mahogany' but in the library 'Light Blue' to 'London Stone', and in the entrance hall 'Fowler Pink' to 'Saxon Green', so I know from first-hand experience how profoundly a simple adjustment from light to dark, from rosy glow to serene green, from summer sky to

THIS PAGE Several years ago, we changed the colour of the large entrance hall from 'Fowler Pink' to 'Saxon Green', which has now become an Archive colour. The woodwork is 'White Tie', a creamy white that seems to suit the age of the house. Through the doorway, the matchboard panelling is 'Mahogany'.

BELOW Glimpsed through a door leading off the entrance hall is my study, painted in 'Fowler Pink' with woodwork in 'Blue Gray'. The Regency sofa is upholstered in ticking, the cushion is by Timney Fowler, and the picture of lilies is one of a set of three photograms by artist Susie Needham.

BELOW RIGHT This upstairs library and study has always been known as 'The Monmouth Room', in commemoration of the time the Duke of Monmouth stayed in the house as

part of his royal progress around the country. The bookshelves made by Peter Bennett are painted 'Old White', the ceiling and cornice are 'White Tie', and the walls are 'London Stone'.

ABOVE RIGHT When the Duke was later arrested and executed as a traitor after the failure of the Monmouth Rebellion, the owners of the house hastily installed a plaster relief coat of arms of King James above the fireplace in the same room to prove their loyalty. But the name of the room lives on.

wet sand, can affect the feel of a space and how different its furnishings look against their new backdrop, such that you inevitably reshuffle them and end up with a completely new look.

We moved from London rather suddenly in 2001, having viewed this house on impulse while staying nearby on holiday. Our daughters were aged 10 and 12, and the elder announced to the owner of the house as we stood chatting in the kitchen after a brief tour that we would 'like to buy it'. Two months later we had moved in, and so began a long, messy restoration that included removing later walls,

taking out leaded lights and having new lead fitted to hold the old window glass, and replacing concrete render with lime mortar. Having restored an old house once before, we tried to enjoy the process, rather than spending months in a state of gritty suspense, always longing for things to be finished.

It is a very satisfying process bringing a house built when Henry VIII was on the throne back to optimal health. It will never be the easiest house to heat; the heavy stone flags are laid straight onto the earth, and double glazing is hard to fit in windows with ancient stone mullions. In winter, we rely on the insulation of thick curtains and thick vests, not to mention sheepskin boots in my case. But in all other ways it is a comfortable and accommodating house, its thick stone walls breathing more easily freed from their outer coating of impermeable cement and inner linings of polystyrene damp-proofing, its huge chimneys opened up again, its flagstones released from layers of lino. The fireplace in

RIGHT The 16th-century fireplace in this bedroom had been blocked in when a later flue from a fireplace in the room below was cut through its back. The walls are 'String', a colour we have used extensively in the house, as it complements the local Beer stone of the fireplaces that are a feature of almost every room.

OPPOSITE ABOVE RIGHT Our younger daughter insisted on an all-white room aged 12. Nine years on, and the 'White Tie' of walls and woodwork has not changed, but colour has crept in. The picture above the bed is a design for a scarf from the 1950s, the quilted silk bedspread is from Malabar in Bridport, and the cushions were made by Miranda Eden using an Osborne & Little fabric.

OPPOSITE BELOW RIGHT Just how far from bright white the paint colour 'White Tie' is can be seen in this bathroom, where white tiling reveals it to be more clotted cream than skimmed milk.

the oak-panelled drawing room is big enough to accommodate enormous chunks of tree, and the Aga in the kitchen chugs away, the tops of its hot plates ideal for ironing damp linen, the surface above its two cooler ovens still a favourite perch for visiting daughters who don't wear vests.

I am fortunate to have a mother who is an antiques dealer, and the house is scattered with pieces she has given us or that we have bought from her over the years. Since there are few things I enjoy more than trawling antiques markets and junk shops, it is also full of 'bargains' – things I have bought

not only because I like them, but also because I imagine I could sell them again for a lot more, but never do.

I have now lived in this house for 11 years – longer than I have lived anywhere before. Sometimes, I feel restless and would like to take on another house. But the impulse usually fades.

DECORATING PRINCIPLE 10

Finishing Touches

Choosing a paint finish is a question of practicality, but it also affects how colour and texture are perceived. The matt, chalky surface of Estate Emulsion and ultra-matt Dead Flat have a depth that is almost tangible. More durable Eggshell, often chosen for woodwork, has a gentle sheen that flatters three-dimensional mouldings. Full Gloss is the toughest and most reflective of all, bouncing light from its surface and highlighting every curve.

ABOVE RIGHT In Antonello Radi's apartment (see pages 162–169), Full Gloss has been used on the walls of a huge, walk-in double shower. Although this is not recommended, it creates a seamless effect where the 'Dimity' Estate Emulsion meets 'Dimity' Full Gloss.

BELOW RIGHT Again, in the full knowledge that it is not recommended, Marco Lobina (see pages 104–111) has chosen to use Dead Flat 'Strong White' for the walls of his kitchen, purely for the aesthetics of its matt, velvety finish.

CENTRE Estate Eggshell has been used for both walls and woodwork in our internal hallway (see pages 170–177). The 'Mahogany' of the walls glimmers as the uneven surface of the old lime plaster is picked up by light slanting across it.

OPPOSITE ABOVE RIGHT The 'Off-Black' Full Gloss of this hall table (see pages 44–51) makes it shine like lacquer.

OPPOSITE BELOW RIGHT James van der Velden (see pages 74–79) wanted to draw attention to the huge ceiling beams in his attic apartment, so painted them 'Pitch Black' Full Gloss against walls of matt 'Setting Plaster' pink.

NEUTRAL GROUPINGS

Farrow & Ball is renowned for its range of neutrals, which are easy on the eye and perfect for creating a look of understated elegance. The following groupings work well as colour schemes in their own right, as well as providing a strong foundation for every other colour on the card.

'Off-White' (3)

Traditional Neutrals

This sophisticated group of neutrals has traditional roots but also works extremely well in contemporary situations. The underlying grey-green tones have a softness that creates a decorative scheme which feels as if it has been there forever.

'Lime White' (1)

'Old White' (4)

Suggested accents:
'Light Gray' (17)
'Mouse's Back' (40)
'Pigeon' (25)
'Brocade' wallpaper BP3208

'Slipper Satin' (2004)

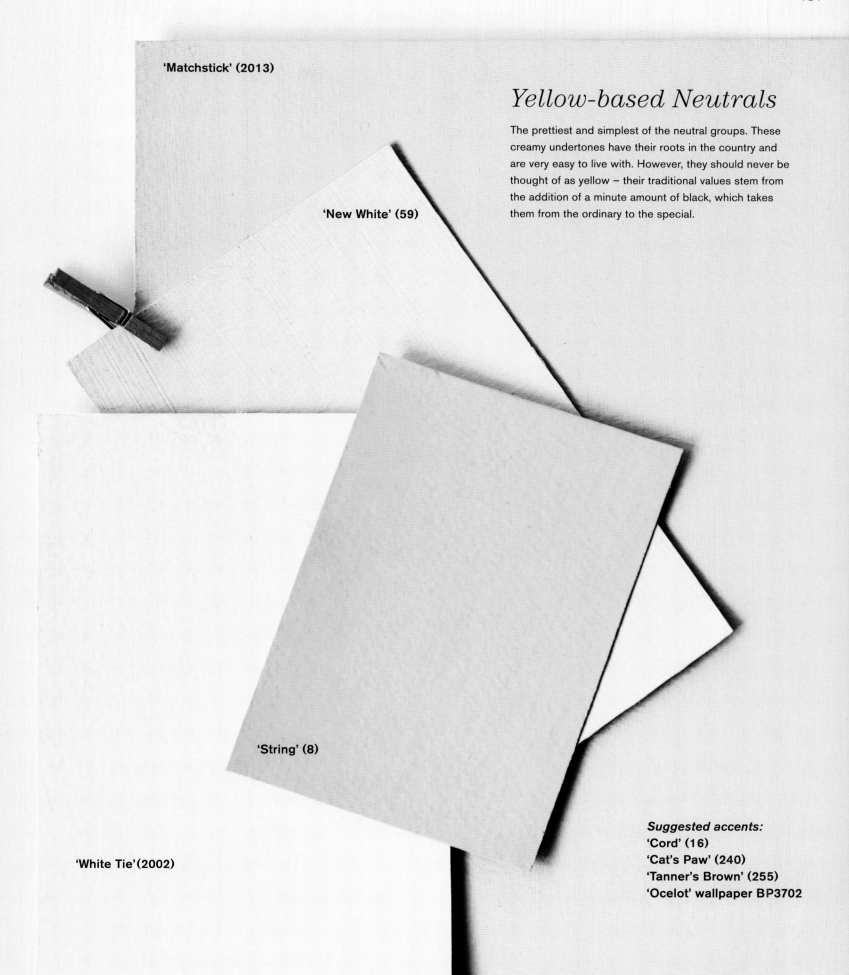

'Matchstick' (2013)

Yellow-based Neutrals

The prettiest and simplest of the neutral groups. These creamy undertones have their roots in the country and are very easy to live with. However, they should never be thought of as yellow – their traditional values stem from the addition of a minute amount of black, which takes them from the ordinary to the special.

'New White' (59)

'String' (8)

'White Tie' (2002)

Suggested accents:
'Cord' (16)
'Cat's Paw' (240)
'Tanner's Brown' (255)
'Ocelot' wallpaper BP3702

Red-based Neutrals

The red base in these ageless neutrals creates
the warmest of all the neutral schemes. They work
beautifully in traditional situations but are also
particularly useful in contemporary homes, being
sympathetic with many materials used today.

Suggested accents:
'London Stone' (6)
'London Clay' (244)
'Eating Room Red' (43)
'Brockhampton Star' wallpaper BP501

'Joa's White' (226)

**'Oxford Stone'
(264)**

**'Pointing'
(2003)**

'Dimity' (2008)

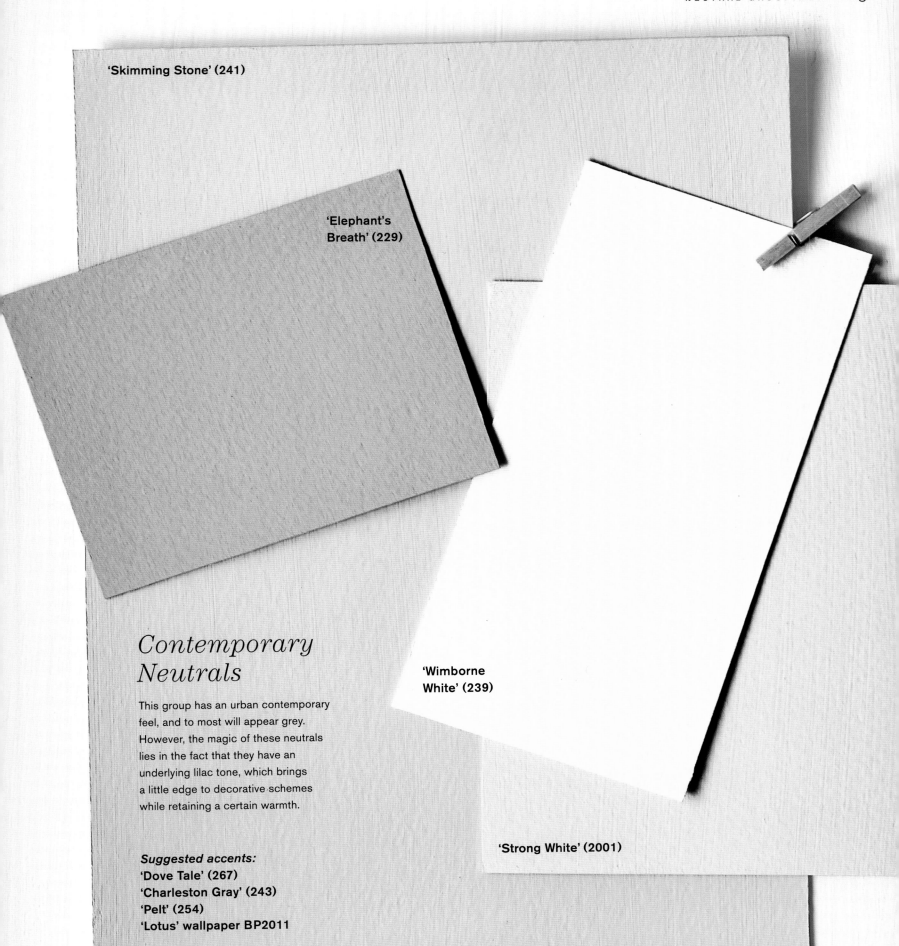

'Skimming Stone' (241)

'Elephant's
Breath' (229)

'Wimborne
White' (239)

'Strong White' (2001)

Contemporary Neutrals

This group has an urban contemporary feel, and to most will appear grey. However, the magic of these neutrals lies in the fact that they have an underlying lilac tone, which brings a little edge to decorative schemes while retaining a certain warmth.

Suggested accents:
'Dove Tale' (267)
'Charleston Gray' (243)
'Pelt' (254)
'Lotus' wallpaper BP2011

Easy Greys

These neutrals have a gossamer appearance that is ideal for those who prefer understated decoration. Neither too cool nor too warm, many people interpret them as the hugely popular tones of the Gustavian period. They are comforting and easy to use.

'Wevet' (273)

'Purbeck Stone' (275)

'Ammonite' (274)

Suggested accents:
'Mole's Breath' (276)
'Railings' (31)
'Stiffkey Blue' (281)
'Tented Stripe' wallpaper ST13113

'Cornforth White' (228)

Architectural Cool

This is the ideal group for those wanting
a strong architectural feel. Purposely cool,
with a bluer undertone than the other groups,
these neutrals create a more hard-edged
look that is conducive to minimal living.

'Plummett' (272)

'Dimpse' (277)

'Pavilion Gray' (242)

'Blackened' (2011)

Suggested accents:
'Down Pipe' (26)
'Railings' (31)
'St Giles Blue' (280)
'Lattice' wallpaper BP3503

PAINTS, PAPERS, AND MORE

These pages introduce and explain the paint finishes and the
artisanal wallpapers used to create the inspiring homes featured
in this book, enabling you to transform your home with colour.

PAINT FINISHES

INTERIOR FINISHES

Estate® Emulsion
This is the most popular paint for walls and ceilings and has the chalky, matt finish and depth of colour so characteristic of Farrow & Ball paints. Despite appearances, it is wipeable.

Modern Emulsion
Also designed for walls and ceilings, this version of emulsion is washable and stain resistant, suitable for kitchens and bathrooms and robust enough for areas of high usage such as hallways. It has a slightly higher sheen than Estate Emulsion.

Estate® Eggshell
Extremely durable and with a low sheen, this is the paint recommended for use on interior woodwork and metalwork, including radiators. It is completely washable.

Full Gloss
A traditional high-gloss finish, versatile and robust enough for both interior and exterior wood and metalwork. It can also be used to dramatic effect on interior walls and ceilings.

Floor Paint
With a mid sheen, this is a very hard-wearing paint that can be used on wooden or concrete floors. It is not suitable for outdoor use.

Dead Flat
This finish is often chosen by purists for the interior of period houses because of its very traditional matt surface that replicates the look of historic lead-based paints. It is wipeable, but not suitable for use in kitchens and bathrooms.

Dead Flat Varnish
Suitable for interior bare wood and painted wood or metal surfaces, this protective varnish has a classic, matt appearance and is wipeable.

Eggshell Varnish
This can be used in exactly the same way as Dead Flat Varnish, but has a low sheen and is washable.

The following specialist finishes, suitable for sympathetic decorating of historic and period homes, are made to order:

Soft Distemper
Made to a traditional recipe using natural resins, this paint has an exceptionally matt and slightly powdery finish and is breathable. It is suitable for walls and ceilings and is only available in the Farrow & Ball range of off-whites.

Casein Distemper
The addition of casein makes this distemper wipeable and more durable than Soft Distemper. It is suitable for walls and ceilings, is breathable and is available in the full range of colours.

Limewash
One of the oldest types of paint, limewash can be used on walls and ceilings both internally and externally. Limewash is available in a selection of Farrow & Ball colours, as indicated on the colour card.

EXTERIOR FINISHES

Exterior Masonry
A very durable matt paint suitable for outside walls, brickwork and render, and available in over 100 colours. It is completely washable.

Exterior Eggshell
Designed for exterior use on softwood and hardwood window frames, cladding, garden furniture, railings, gates and guttering, with a high resistance to flaking and peeling.

WALLPAPER

Richly historical, inherently unique and timelessly beautiful, Farrow & Ball wallpapers stand alone. Created using real Farrow & Ball paints printed onto paper according to artisanal techniques, the wallpapers have an irresistibly tactile texture and unmatchable appearance.

All papers have a 'ground' colour applied with a hand-brushing technique, building the depth and texture of the paper from the beginning. The pattern is then applied using age-old block printing or trough printing methods to apply paint to paper. Stripes, striés, damasks, geometrics and floral designs are lovingly created by skilled craftsmen whose passion and dedication is evident in every roll. In total, more than 300 wallpapers are available in colourways ranging from neutrals to brights and even glimmering metallics, meaning there is a paper to suit every decorating style.

No matter where in the world the wallpaper is hung, every single roll is still made, wrapped, and packed at the same workshop in Dorset, England where the company began. There is no minimum order and you can request up to five free A4 samples.

PRIMERS AND UNDERCOATS

Created using the same natural ingredients and rich pigments as the paints, Farrow & Ball make a complete range of primers and undercoats for use both inside and outside the home.

Every primer and undercoat prepares the surface for painting, giving a smooth, long-lasting finish that can be admired for years to come. From rust-inhibiting Metal Primer & Undercoat and Wood Knot & Resin Blocking Primer, to Wall & Ceiling Primer & Undercoat, the range is available in four colours designed to work with your chosen paint colour. The correct undercoat for every shade can be found on the Farrow & Ball colour card or on the website.

ARCHIVE

If you truly love a colour, you'll never want to use another. At Farrow & Ball there are only ever 132 colours on the colour card. Over the years, some colours have been superseded by newer ones, but a colour is never discontinued. Instead, it is affectionately described as 'retiring' to the Archive, where it forever remains available to order.

Similarly, Farrow & Ball wallpapers are available in an edited selection of colourways, but there are more than 1000 different combinations available from the Archive that can be specially printed for you on request.

HOW TO ORDER

Most paint can be purchased and taken away from Farrow & Ball showrooms and stockists throughout the world. Visit www.farrow-ball.com for an up-to-date list of retailers in your area. Every paint colour and finish or any wallpaper design can also be purchased through the Farrow & Ball website or through our mail-order service.

For advice on paint, wallpaper, and choosing colours, either visit your nearest Farrow & Ball showroom or stockist or contact Farrow & Ball directly on +44 (0)1202 876141 (UK, Europe and rest of world) or 1 888 511 1121 (North America).

PICTURE CREDITS

All photography by Jan Baldwin

Endpapers: 'Renaissance' wallpaper BP2809; **1** The home of the writer Ros Byam Shaw in Devon; **2** The home of Karina, Victor and George Bjerregaard Chen in Denmark; **3** The home of designer Anne-Marie Midy and Jorge Almada of Casamidy in Paris; **4** John Nicolson's house is available as a film and photographic location; **5 above left** 'La Maison du College Royal'; **5 above right** Gisbert Pöppler Architektur Interieur; **5 below right** A Dutch farmhouse designed by Jan and Maud Steengracht van Oostcapelle-Noltes; **6** The home of interior designer Antonello Radi in Foligno, Italy; **7** A Dutch farmhouse designed by Jan and Maud Steengracht van Oostcapelle-Noltes; **8 above** John Nicolson's house is available as a film and photographic location; **8 below** The home of the interior designer Eva Gnaedinger in Switzerland; **9** The home of the writer Ros Byam Shaw in Devon; **10–11** Gisbert Pöppler Architektur Interieur; **12** The home of Maria and Frank in Southern Germany, with interior design by Barbara G; **13** Gisbert Pöppler Architektur Interieur; **14–24** The home of Maria and Frank in Southern Germany, with interior design by Barbara G; **24 right–25** The home of the interior designer Eva Gnaedinger in Switzerland; **25 above right** John Nicolson's house is available as a film and photographic location; **25 below right** Home of James van der Velden, owner of design studio Bricks Amsterdam, the Netherlands; **26–33** John Nicolson's house is available as a film and photographic location; **34–41** Kristin Krogstad Interior Architect, www.thedrawingroom.no; **42–43 above left** The home of Maria and Frank in Southern Germany, with interior design by Barbara G; **42 below left** John Nicolson's house is available as a film and photographic location; **42–43 below** Kristin Krogstad Interior Architect, www.thedrawingroom.no; **43 right** John Nicolson's house is available as a film and photographic location; **44–51** The home of Karina, Victor and George Bjerregaard Chen in Denmark; **52–61** Gisbert Pöppler Architektur Interieur; **62 above** The home of the interior designer Eva Gnaedinger in Switzerland; **62 below** The home of designer Anne-Marie Midy and Jorge Almada of Casamidy in Paris; **63** Gisbert Pöppler Architektur Interieur; **64–70** The London home of Mr and Mrs David Smith, designed by Emma Burns of Sibyl Colefax & John Fowler; **71 above centre** The home of Sophie Lambert, owner of Au Temps des Cerises in France; **71 above right** La Maison du College Royal; **71 below centre** The home of the interior designer Eva Gnaedinger in Switzerland; **71 below right** 'La Maison du College Royal'; **72** The home of the interior designer Eva Gnaedinger in Switzerland; **73** A Roman interior by Andrea Truglio; **74–79** Home of James van der Velden, owner of design studio Bricks Amsterdam, the Netherlands; **80–85** The home of designer Anne-Marie Midy and Jorge Almada of Casamidy in Paris; **86–93** Designer Laure Vial du Chatenet from Maison Caumont Paris; **94 above left** Kristin Krogstad Interior Architect, www.thedrawingroom.no; **94 below left** A Dutch farmhouse designed by Jan and Maud Steengracht van Oostcapelle-Noltes; **94–95** The home of Sophie Lambert, owner of Au Temps des Cerises in France; **95 above right** A Dutch farmhouse designed by Jan and Maud Steengracht van Oostcapelle-Noltes; **95 below right** Designer Laure Vial du Chatenet from Maison Caumont Paris; **96–103** The home of the interior designer Eva Gnaedinger in Switzerland; **104–107** Marco Lobina's home in Turin; **112–113 above** The London home of Mr and Mrs David Smith, designed by Emma Burns of Sibyl Colefax & John Fowler; **112 below left** The home of Maria and Frank in Southern Germany, with interior design by Barbara G; **113 below left** Kristin Krogstad Interior Architect, www.thedrawingroom.no; **113 right** A Dutch farmhouse designed by Jan and Maud Steengracht van Oostcapelle-Noltes; **114–121** A Roman interior by Andrea Truglio; **122–123 above left & below left** A Roman interior by Andrea Truglio; **122–123 below centre** The home of designer Anne-Marie Midy and Jorge Almada of Casamidy in Paris; **123 right** The home of interior designer Antonello Radi in Foligno, Italy; **124–131** A Dutch farmhouse designed by Jan and Maud Steengracht van Oostcapelle-Noltes; **132–141** 'La Maison du College Royal'; **142 above left** Kristin Krogstad Interior Architect, www.thedrawingroom.no; **142 below left** John Nicolson's house is available as a film and photographic location; **142–143 centre & above right** La Maison du College Royal; **143 below right** The home of the interior designer Eva Gnaedinger in Switzerland; **144–151** Kristin Krogstad Interior Architect, www.thedrawingroom.no; **152–159** The home of Sophie Lambert, owner of Au Temps des Cerises in France; **160–161 above left** La Maison du College Royal; **161 below left** The home of the writer Ros Byam Shaw in Devon; **160–161 below centre** 'La Maison du College Royal'; **161 right** The home of Sophie Lambert, owner of Au Temps des Cerises in France; **162–169** The home of interior designer Antonello Radi in Foligno, Italy; **170–177** The home of the writer Ros Byam Shaw in Devon; **178 above left** The home of interior designer Antonello Radi in Foligno, Italy; **179 below left** Marco Lobina's home in Turin; **178–179 centre** The home of the writer Ros Byam Shaw in Devon; **179 above right** The home of Karina, Victor and George Bjerregaard Chen in Denmark; **179 below right** Home of James van der Velden, owner of design studio Bricks Amsterdam, the Netherlands; **187 left** The home of interior designer Antonello Radi in Foligno, Italy; **187 centre** The London home of Mr and Mrs David Smith, designed by Emma Burns of Sibyl Colefax & John Fowler; **187 right** A Dutch farmhouse designed by Jan and Maud Steengracht van Oostcapelle-Noltes; **192** The home of Sophie Lambert, owner of Au Temps des Cerises in France.

BUSINESS CREDITS

Architects, artists, designers and businesses whose work and homes have been featured in this book:

CASAMIDY
Pila Seca 3
San Miguel de Allende
GTO 37700
Mexico
and at
108 Avenue Moliere
1190 Brussels
Belgium
T: 32 (02) 345 2553
E: casamidy@casamidy.com
www.casamidy.com
Pages 3; 62 below; 80–85,
122–123 below centre.

EMMA BURNS OF
SIBYL COLEFAX & JOHN FOWLER
Sibyl Colefax & John Fowler
39 Brook Street
London W1K 4JE
T: +44 (0)20 7493 2231
E: decorators@sibylcolefax.com
www.sibylcolefax.com
Pages 64–70, 112–113 above,
187 centre.

EVA GNAEDINGER
www.evagnaedinger.com
Pages 8 below, 24 right, 25, 62 above,
71 below, 72, 96–103, 143 below right.

BARBARA GÜGEL
Architect
Dipl.-Ing.(univ)
Barbara Gügel
Kesslestrasse 10
96047 Bamberg
Bayern
Germany
T: +49 (0)951 3094514
info@lebenswert-bamberg.de
www.lebenswert-bamberg.de
Pages12, 14–24, 42–43 above left,
112 below left.

KRISTIN KROGSTAD
Kristin Krogstad Interior Architect
T: +47 (0)92666005
E: Kristin@thedrawingroom.no
www.thedrawingroom.no
Pages 34–41, 42–42 below, 94 above left,
113 below left, 142 above left, 144–151.

SOPHIE LAMBERT:
Au Temps des Cerises
22 rue du Vieil Abreuvoir
78100 St Germain en Laye
France
T: +33 (0)139734192
www.deco-autempsdescerises.com
Pages 71 above, 94–95, 152–159,
161 right, 192.

MARCO LOBINA
www.rezina.it
www.uda.it
Pages 104–107, 179 below left.

LA MAISON DU COLLEGE ROYAL
Available to rent for weekends
and holidays.
T: +33 (0)6 13 23 35 78
E: juliettebartillat@free.fr
www.lamaisonducollegeroyal.com
Pages 5 above left, 71 above right,
132–141, 142–143 centre & right,
160–161 above left, 160–161
below centre.

JOHN NICOLSON:
E: johnnynicolson@aol.com
and
Landscape Architect:
Luis Buitrago, M.L.Arch
E: Lmbuitrago@aol.com
Pages 4, 8 above, 25 above right, 26–33,
42 below, 43 right, 142 below left.

GISBERT PÖPPLER
Architektur Interieur
Falckensteinstrasse 48
D-10997 Berlin
T: +49 (0)30 44044973
E: mail@gisbertpoeppler.com
www.gisbertpoeppler.com
also featuring
Kitchen artwork by 22quadrat
Denis Vidinski & Patrick Voigt
Wörthstrasse 56
49082 Osnabrück
T: +49 (0)541 3326813
E: info@22quadrat.com
www.22quadrat.com
Pages 5 above right, 10–11, 13, 52–61.

ANTONELLO RADI
Interior Designer (Italy/
New York)
T: +39 (0)328 894 3203

E: a.radi@aleteia.com
Pages 6, 63, 123 right, 162–169,
178 above left, 187 left.

MAUD STEENGRACHT VAN
OOSTCAPELLE-NOLTES
Interior Decorator
Maud Steengracht van
Oostcapelle-Noltes
T: +31 (0)654362216
E; maud@steengrachtartware.com
www.steengrachtartware.com
also featuring
Iron Design Lighting and Furniture
Jan Steengracht van Oostcapelle
T: +31 (0)654796585
E: jan@steengrachtartware.com
www.steengrachtartware.com
and
Etching in kitchen by Sophie Steengracht
van Oostcapelle
http://cargocollective.com/soof
http://society6.com/subtlemovement
Farrow & Ball paints from
INTERFURN (Farrow & Ball Holland)
Ron Zaal – Agent/importer
T: +31 (0)79 3600307
www.interfurn.nl
Pages 5 below right, 7, 94 below left,
95 above right, 113 right, 124–131,
187 right.

ANDREA TRUGLIO
E: andreatruglio@yahoo.it
www.andreatruglio.com
Pages 73, 114–121, 122–123 above left
& below left.

JAMES VAN DER VELDEN
Bricks Amsterdam
T: +31 (0)621201272
E: info@bricks-amsterdam.com
www.bricksamsterdam.com
Pages 25 below right, 74–79,
179 below right.

LAURE VIAL DE CHATENET
Maison Caumont Paris
Showroom at
10–12 rue Pierre Picard
75018 Paris
France
T: +33 (0)1 83 87 98 01
www.maisoncaumont.com
Pages 86–93, 95 below right.

INDEX Page numbers in *italic* refer to illustrations and their captions

ACKNOWLEDGMENTS

First and foremost, I would like to thank the team at Farrow & Ball for the time, effort, and thought they have applied to the production of this book, for their help providing important contacts, and for infecting everyone with enthusiasm for their products. I would particularly like to thank Sarah Cole, their Marketing Director, whose input has been invaluable, and expert Colour Consultant Joa Studholme.

Any book is a team effort, but only a couple of people at most are credited on its cover. In this instance they are me as writer, and Jan Baldwin, who took the photographs, carried more than her fair share of the heavy bags of equipment, and was generally the best travelling companion anyone could hope for. Jan is not only a superb photographer, she is also a pleasure to work with. But Jan and I are just the tip of the iceberg. None of our trips to locations all over Europe would have been possible without the inspired research and excellent organization of Jess Walton at Ryland Peters & Small. Without her, there would be no book. I am also extremely grateful for the support of Publishing Director Cindy Richards, who helped to originate the idea for the book, of Leslie Harrington, the Art Director, and of Publicity Manager Lauren Wright. My thanks are likewise due to Production Controller Gordana Simakovic, who has worked so hard to ensure that colour reproduction is accurate, and to Toni Kay, who has designed the book so beautifully. Annabel Morgan is a wonderful editor and, like the best kind of parent, doles out as much encouragement and advice as she does reminders of deadlines.